图书在版编目（CIP）数据

中国东西：英文 / 波普客编著. –– 北京：五洲传播出版社, 2008.7
(2013.7重印)
ISBN 978-7-5085-1280-8

Ⅰ. ①中… Ⅱ. ①波… Ⅲ. ①生活－基本知识－中国－英文 Ⅳ.
①TS97

中国版本图书馆CIP数据核字(2013)第130457号

中国元素系列丛书

中国东西

波普客 编著

丛书主编：吴学夫
策划编辑：荆孝敏
文　　字：李日松　吴学夫
翻　　译：刘　浚
摄　　影：邹盛武　曹雪风
装帧设计：黄云蔚

责任编辑：张美景

出版发行：五洲传播出版社
地　　址：北京市海淀区北三环中路31号凯奇大厦B座7层
邮　　编：100088
电　　话：010-82001477
传　　真：010-82001477
网　　址：http://www.cicc.org.cn/
开　　本：787x 1092mm　1/16
印　　张：11
版　　次：2008年7月第1版　2013年8月第5次印刷
印　　刷：北京华彩盛业印刷有限公司
书　　号：ISBN 978-7-5085-1280-8
定　　价：99元

CHINESE STUFF

波普客**POPcorn**

Translated by Liu Jun

China Intercontinental Press

Contents

Preface

Ordinary articles in common use in China by the largest population in the world have already become symbolized objects. But how many people, to be exact, have ever noticed their cultural values? If every article has its objective denotation and connotation, then tens of thousands of Chinese stuff must have cohered into a unique cultural system beyond their own physical properties, a system of objects which is infused with psychic energy and possesses cultural properties.

Development of technologies and global trade have created a tendency of homogeneity of life of people around the world but there are also loads of common articles still full of vitality in daily life of people, which embody national individualities. In China, we are not inclined to exhibit Chinese-style stuff which have been already classified into a historical category or as specimens of folk customs, neither are we willing to show great and glorious symbols, such as the Four Great Inventions. What we are looking for are the stuff that are commonly seen and being in use in China, from which we scrutinously appreciate the aesthetics of everyday life. We believe it is these pristine Chinese-style stuff that reflect the aesthetic consciousness of the country and its people. Seemingly, a lot of Chinese-style stuff have abandoned sophisticated techniques, enduring quality and decent appearances but the political, economic and cultural backgrounds hiding behind this coarse and lovely Chinese-style aesthetics are just what we must notice. When artists and designers from China are engaged in global competition according to international practices and standards, what we should be mostly clear about are the stance that we take and reality that we are in.

Except for the features of aesthetics, the Chinese-style stuff for show in this book are also characterized by some interesting traits: intense ethnic preferences, improvise-ism, mixing of pragmatism, flexible accommodability, political tradition & legacy and gene of social system as well as mental state of show-off and affectation... We extract Chinese-style stuff from their ecological environments for an in-depth scrutiny of structural contexts and cultural connotations of the things themselves, trying to decipher the relationships between the stuff and the Chinese people and between them and the Chinese society.

Why attention on contemporaneous articles in common use in China? For China whose influences to the world have been increasingly profound, we cannot present it to the world only with its serious politics, stereo-type historical specimens or grand epic image of elitism. Instead, we hope to explore cultural values in pristineness and humanity manifested by concrete objects of everyday life (i.e. articles, architecture, imagery, men or women) and exhibit a live and animated China to the whole world.

Wu Xuefu

Office & Classroom
文房礼仪

Brown envelope | Iron clip | Writing exercises book | Embroidered banner | *Xinhua Dictionary* |
Exercises books with checked paper | Train ticket | Name plates | Abacus | Cankao Xiaoxi (Reference News) |
Wenquxing Electronic Dictionary | Certificate of merit for "Three-Good Student" | Official seal | 100-yuan note |
Invoice | Banknote verification machine | Pulled school bag | Business calendar

Brown envelope

33x24x3cm
Kraft paper, String

The brown envelope contains a person's identity and other records. But the person can never open his or her own file, which is mysterious as the black box on a plane. Every Chinese has such a file envelope containing yellowing pages that keep record of the person's life. Coming from the traditional household registration system, the brown envelope is still an important way through which the government rules the country. Ever since a person's birth, major happenings in one's life are filed away in this envelope. There are questions like: From which date to which date, where did you study or work? Are you politically progressive? Who are related with you? The brown envelopes are sealed and stored in a dark room. Nowadays, Chinese still rely on the ID card and household registration card to prove their identities. But occasionally, they also need the brown envelope to prove their innocence. For decades, the brown envelope has maintained its humble appearance. Even in the time of digital information, a person's crucial records are still stored in this ordinary envelope. Everyone has such an envelope, but how much is the file related with the person's actual life?

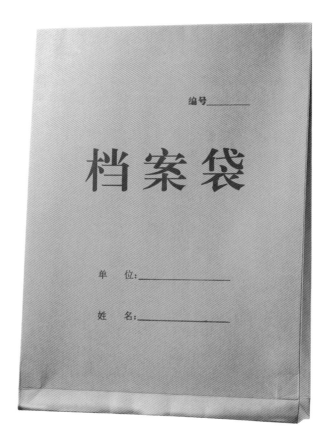

Iron clip

6.2x6x3.3cm
Iron

With a heavy paper board and two iron clips, Xiao Wang began painting. She is now a teacher in an art school. Whenever she thinks about the days she spent painting in the children's palace, the two used iron clips always come to her mind. The iron clip is a common stationery item in Chinese offices. The bigger ones are used to bind newspapers and the smaller ones clip invoices. But besides the common functions, some clips are used in imaginative ways. Master Li puts a clip on his nose while sleeping, for he believes this can stop his thunder-like snoring. Many families clip the mosquito incense, which stops burning at the iron clip, so the incense can be used next time. Zhang Jianjun, a soldier, uproots unwanted moustache with a clip. Before colorful plastic clips become popular, housewives often sealed bags of food with iron clip. In the past, department stores in small counties had iron wires linking the cashier and the counters. There were many iron clips on the web of wires. The shop assistants would bind cash and receipts on the iron clips and throw them towards the cashier. The cashier, usually a woman, took the cash, got the change and wrote the invoice, then bound them on the clip and threw it back in a precise and elegant manner. The iron clips are very strong. Once it gets hold on something, it seldom lets the object loose. At times when materials and chances were scant, the spirit of the iron clip was a virtue for those who were eager to hold on to opportunities, ideals and a better future.

Writing
exercises book

26x18.5x0.2cm
Paper

When Chinese children begin learning calligraphy, they have to struggle with the painting brush held vertically in their small hands. The writing exercises book has proven to be a very patient and effective teacher. Printed with the strokes of Chinese characters in light red ink, the exercises book enables children to navigate their brush along the correct order. "A person's handwriting is a true mirror of one's character," teachers and parents often say this to children, as if someone who has a good handwriting is guaranteed for high esteem in the society. Old Wang often points at the writing by officials and warns his child that no matter how prominent an official is, the poor handwriting will let him down and lose face in public. The child understands little of this teaching, but has to continue working on the exercises book. In China and abroad, in history and at present, bibliotists have devoted themselves to the study of handwriting. Today, when urban students attend computer lessons at the first grade, parents have to make extra efforts to let their juniors understand the importance of calligraphy. Thanks to modern technology, one can input a long Chinese article in the computer with a variety of software and change the characters into any writing style available in the database. But there are some people who still believe in the merits of writing with a brush. That's why writing exercises books are still in good demand and printed with various styles left by ancient calligraphers.

Embroidered banner

96x72.2x8cm
Fabric, Wood, Plastic

When the Chinese want to express their gratitude in the most respectful manner, they would present a banner embroidered with the praise. It is common to find such banners in the meeting room of many "units", a term referring to the place where a Chinese works. Every time a meeting is held, the staff will be surrounded by banners showcasing the unit's awards and praises. The government grants banners to outstanding figures in certain areas; the common people also like to use this means to show their respect or gratitude. The same banner can be used among different levels of social status. The words are often succinct when the banner is given as an award. For instance, "The 2nd Class of Grade 3 in the high school has won First Prize in the tug-of-war contest", or "Zhang Weihong is honored as the role model of spiritual civilization". But the eloquence can be surprising in the event of expressing utmost gratitude. A patient might present a doctor with a banner that says: "Hua Tuo (an ancient doctor) reborn, bringing back spring with wonderful hands" as shown in the picture, or "Virtuous doctor who helps the needed with great skills". A student might give his or her alma mater a banner that praises the school as "spring breezes that bring timely rain to nurture the earth silently". People often send banners to governmental agencies with gratitude. For example, they would praise the police as "brave and fearless, with a great social conscience", or "good police for the people, guardians of life". For the governmental agency that alleviates disaster-stricken areas, the people would say "sending charcoals in snow, bright sun in winter". There are numerous such praises, which are often arranged in antithetical couplets. For Chinese, things in even number are considered perfect.

赠一汽公交巴士车队黄洪民司机

拾金不昧品德高
热情服务情义深

乘客林良园敬赠
二零一一年三月

Xinhua Dictionary

13.2x10x3cm
Paper, Plastic

To Chinese learning their language, *Xinhua Dictionary* is like a Bible. First published by The Commercial Press in 1953, the small dictionary has influenced several generations. Each character is arranged according to its pronunciation in pinyin and explained in detail, with succinct examples. The 10th edition, published in 2003, has been sold for some 400 million copies. Some sources say it is the most widely used dictionary in the whole world. From professors to taxi drivers, almost every Chinese resorts to the dictionary when they aren't sure of a word's meaning or pronunciation. Fan Wei, a rickshaw driver in Anshan, China's Liaoning province, has memorized every word of the dictionary that has more than 500 pages and some 9,000 entries. The "living dictionary" can tell the page, line and explanation of every character. Old Wang, a retired worker, always keeps a *Xinhua Dictionary* by his pillow. The dictionary that has accompanied him since the apprentice days has rippling cover and curled pages. Some people say that an ordinary man is just like a *Xinhua Dictionary* – it is easy to understand and always at hand; it is the best companion in a person's life.

Exercises books with checked paper

17.6x12.7x0.15cm
Paper

There are just a few countries in the world where students use exercises books with checked paper, but there are more students in the world learning to write in this way. Every Chinese student begins writing with such exercises books. The small checks carry the structure, mobility and essence of written Chinese characters. Mr Zheng recalls that in his childhood, he often thought about games while writing on the exercises books. "I didn't see that the characters were running out of the checks, until my dad hit me suddenly on the head. He would order me to rip off the page and rewrite everything." Like Mr Zheng, many people remember the dull afternoons and even late nights when they had to copy an article for some five or ten times as a punishment for their naughty deeds. Once a clever boy put some carbon paper between several pages to copy the text. But the teacher discovered the trick and displayed the exercises book in the class. Everyone had a hearty laugh, except for the poor boy. Young Chinese born in the 1980s have learned writing with the computer. They are amazing at sending mobile phone messages with *pinyin*. But the speedy input software has alienated the younger generation from writing. Some of them have neglected differences in homophones and even made fun of the words. It is a pity that the beauty of written Chinese characters that has inspired ancient calligraphy is not gaining wide appreciation as before.

Train ticket

9x6x0.1cm
Paper

Decades ago, train tickets were small pieces of hard paper at half the size of a name card. Today, a thin piece of paper doubling the original size is printed at ticket windows linked with the national network. What makes the train ticket special in China is the Spring Festival, the most important traditional festival in the country when everyone is supposed to go home for family reunion. Chinese pay utmost attention to the banquet on the Eve of the lunar New Year that usually falls in late January or early February. As millions of students who begin their winter vacation in January join migrant workers who are eager to bring cash to their rural home, the world's biggest traffic must be achieved in a matter of days. A train ticket, though priced just a few hundred yuan for a distance of thousands of kilometers, is hard to get. Chen Chao, who had found a reliable source to get the ticket, was let down at the last moment. The young man searched online and finally discovered a compatriot who was selling the ticket as he couldn't go home. But Chen had to spend the New Year's Eve on the train. He felt very sad in the empty train, listening to firecrackers along the way. But in a way, Chen didn't have to endure the crowds. Those who only have a ticket for standing room are forced to remain immobile for hours, as every corner of the train is stuffed with people. In the long journey, it is almost impossible to get to the toilet, which is often congested despite the smell. Some ingenious businessmen have made good profits selling diapers for grown ups. It is safe to say that train ride is a pleasant journey in the country most time of the year. But be prepared for some extremes, should you plan a trip around the major holidays such as the Spring Festival and National Holiday (on October 1).

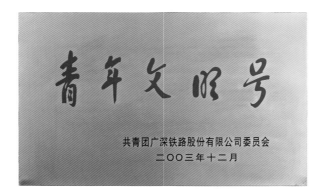

Name plates

48x30x2.5cm
Copper

It is common to see one or more plates outside the gate of a unit, or the departments and sections of a unit. The plate carries the title of the unit, or awards such as "Advanced Unit", "Civilized Unit" or "AAAA Level Unit". Mostly made of stainless steel or copper, the rectangular plates are sometimes gilded with gold or silver, and the characters are usually inscribed in formal boldface or regular script. Judging from the material, shape and technique, the plates seem to have come from the same mould. However, the titles or honors on the apparently solid plates don't always match the reality. There was an academic society that made a good profit by selling copper plates saying "Cooperation Unit with the Chinese XXX Society" to whichever shops willing to pay the price. When this was disclosed by the media, there was much public outcry against it. There is another nuisance for the plate – it seems to be very attractive to thieves, who often carry them away for a lucrative price at the recycling stations.

Abacus

27.5x13x2cm
Wood, Copper

Abacus is an ancient calculating device invented in China. In the famous long painting scroll titled *Along the River on the Pure Brightness Festival (Qingming Shang He Tu)*, Northern Song Dynasty (960-1279) painter Zhang Zeduan depicted hundreds of people doing various businesses along the Bianhe River in the empire's capital Bianliang (today's Kaifeng of Henan province). In a drugstore, an abacus is seen on the counter. The abacus is a traditional symbol of business acumen. Many domestic films and TV dramas would give a close-up shot of an abacus, then slowly pulls out to reveal the accountant wearing a skullcap and a pair of glasses that has slid to the tip of the nose. In a drugstore smelling of the sweet and bitter traditional Chinese medicine, the druggist can be seen holding the steelyard in one hand and clicking away on the abacus on the other. In Sidney Sheldon's novel *If Tomorrow Comes*, when Jeff promotes a "mini-calculator", he says it is "absolutely reasonable, free of errors, energy-saving and requires no maintenance in ten years". It turns out that the "mini-calculator" is an abacus from China.

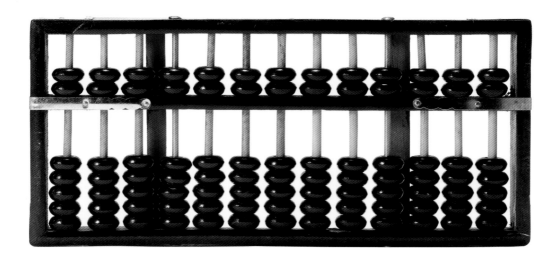

Cankao Xiaoxi (Reference News)

28x20x0.7cm
Paper

Cankao Xiaoxi (Reference News) is only distributed in China, but it enjoys a circulation of 3 million. With 36 printing spots, the daily paper can reach most of its readers across the country on time. Most stories are translated and edited from foreign news agencies, as well as sources from Taiwan, Macao and Hong Kong. The reports offer different angles and styles from those of domestic news stories. Before the Internet became popular, Reference News was a window through which Chinese caught a glimpse of the rest of the world. Founded in 1931, Reference News was a confidential report for Mao Zedong, Zhou Enlai and other leaders of the Chinese Communist Party. In 1957, it became a newspaper and reached more readers. But for decades, reading the Reference News would remain a privilege of the influential people.

Wenquxing Electronic Dictionary

11.4x8.4x1.7cm
Plastic, PCB, etc.

Wenquxing is a legendary god in charge of imperial examinations and literary affairs. More than a decade ago, an electronic dictionary manufacturer used it to name its product. If you search "Wenquxing" on baidu.com, the Chinese equivalent of Google, most of the entries that appear will be this electronic dictionary. As the craze of learning English sweeps through the country, the dictionary is gaining popularity in the same way as is the classic *Xinhua Dictionary* about Chinese language. The electronic dictionary has been updated constantly to meet the customers' needs. While students and white collars struggle to pass various tests for English level certificates, bilingual kindergartens are mushrooming in the country. A teacher said: "I'm studying ancient Chinese written language. To get the professional title of professor, I must attend the national English level test. This is really puzzling."

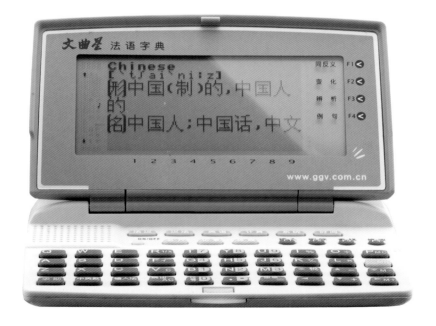

Certificate of merit for "Three-Good Student"

38.4x26.6x0.1cm
Paper

"Three-Good Student" is the most coveted honor for Chinese students and their aspiring parents. Liu Yafei, a diligent student, has been gaining such honor every year since primary school. Her parents put up all her awards on the most prominent wall in the sitting room. Every visitor would praise the girl and her parents heartily. Occasionally, a guest would go home to reprimand his or her less diligent child and promise to reward the child if he or she gains such a certificate. The "Three Goods" refer to "virtue, intelligence and physical health". It is intended for those who are balanced in all three respects. But in reality, most parents and teachers only focus on the second standard, or the scores of examinations. Practiced for many years in China, such a system has met increasing criticism. More and more people believe that better ways should be found to develop a student's full potentials, especially when a student couldn't meet the traditional standards of the "Three-Good Student".

Official seal

4x4x5.5cm
Red gum

In 2007, the remote Guiye village in Jinping county of Southwest China's Guizhou province caught national fame when villagers divided an official seal into five parts. Four village representatives and a member of the village committee each holds a part of the seal that is engraved with the words "Approved by Villagers' Financial Team, Guiye village, Pingqiu town". When the village plans on an expenditure, it needs at least three seal-holders' agreement before the seal is put together and the spending can be approved. When publicized by the media, this seal is dubbed as "the most powerful official seal in Chinese history". It is said that no villager has ever doubted how the village committee uses their money since the seal was divided. Official seal is very powerful in China. Every Chinese will encounter the day when getting a seal of approval is as hard as climbing into the clouds. Sometimes, one needs to reach some 100 government departments for a seal of approval before achieving anything. In a gesture of serving the people, the government has offered the so-called "all-in-all service". In a spacious hall, one can get all the signatures from various agencies in a matter of hours. The official seal is a symbol of power. In this respect, it reminds people of the emperors' imperial seals that were generally made of jade. There have been many reports about frauds involving fake seals. One story goes that a man solicited marriage in a TV program. At the end of his love letter, he would affix an official seal from a certain unit where he said he was working. Several women were cheated by this simple trick, proving the power of the seal.

100-yuan note

15.5x7.5cm
Cotton paper

In the fifth set of RMB banknotes, the red 100-yuan note is the most jubilant. Chinese people love red. This note is given this color also because it is of the highest value among all banknotes. Each set of banknotes is an epitome of its time. The face value, color, patterns and other elements not only show the country's economic condition, but also the aesthetic preferences of the time. The first set of RMB was issued in 1948 before the People's Republic of China was founded. There are many printed versions of different technical levels. It reflects how the country was just recovering from decades of war. The second set of RMB issued in 1962 features automobile, plane, ship, tractor, train and hydro power station, providing glimpses of busy reconstruction throughout the nation. The third set issued soon afterwards added more scenes showing farmers and workers. The color and frame are more harmonious. The fourth set of RMB issued in 1984 was a fundamental improvement. The newly added 50-yuan and 100-yuan notes directly show the advances of Chinese economy. The 100-yuan note shows national founders Mao Zedong, Zhou Enlai, Liu Shaoqi and Zhu De. The 50-yuan note shows three figures representing workers, farmers and intellectuals. The other notes show 14 ethnic minorities. All figures are realistic portraits. The fifth set of RMB issued in 1999 is more internationalized. The portrait of Chairman Mao Zedong became the uniform pattern on the front side of all banknotes. People love this smiling face, not only out of respect for the founder of New China, but also due to a common love and pursuit of better life.

Invoice

11x8x0.1cm, etc.
Paper

Invoice is a proof of purchasing a commodity or receiving a service. It normally records the name and price of the commodity, as well as the time and location of the purchase. More importantly, it is recognized in law and tax. Chinese people pay great attention to invoice. The consumers would ask for an invoice, which is indispensable if they want to return or repair the commodity. Many units ask their employees to provide invoices to prove their spending was reasonable and in the interests of the unit. The government controls taxes through the invoice. There are hand-written and printed invoices. Some invoices carry an award bar. When you scrape off the silver covering on the bar, you can see if you've won an award, which is generally a few yuan. The lucky ones can cash in from the seller immediately. This is a devise by the government to encourage people to ask for invoices.

此发票系北京市地方税务局批准印制·21·09·06
Printing of the invoice is ratified by Beijing Local Taxation Bureau

北京市定额专用发票
BEIJING QUOTA SPECIAL INVOICE

发票联
INVOICE

发票代码
Invoice code   211000902070

发票号码
Invoice No   01348954

密　　码
Password

信息码
INF .number   2007090102

10090207-04201133-48954775

壹拾元   ￥：10.00
Ten yuan

税号：H0222762151550

发票专用章

开票日期   年　月　日   收款单位（盖章有效）
Date issued   Y M D   Payee (seal)

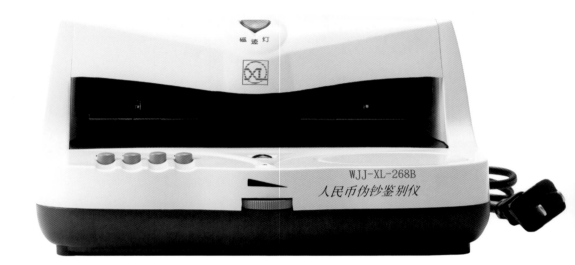

Banknote verification machine

21.8x16.3x11cm
Plastic, Metal

On the counter of banks and department stores, you can find typewriter-sized machines that verify banknotes. Equipped with ultraviolet rays and magnetic sensing, the machines would count the number of banknotes and reject suspicious ones. Some machines would even announce in a woman's voice: "This is a false note." All bank clerks process 100-yuan notes with the machine. It is ruled by the government that false notes are confiscated upon discovery. Forgers have tried many ways to deceit the clerks and machines. One forger separated the front and back of a real note successfully and stuck them with false sides. Although he cheated some machines, this forgery was disclosed soon.

Pulled school bag

53.3x35x23cm
Plastic, Metal, Fabric

In the morning, if you happen to pass by an elementary school, you might be surprised that many students drag luggage toward school. The luggage, or pulled school bag, doesn't contain travel necessities, instead they are full of books and stationery. A parent said that he once weighed his child's bag and found it was 5 kg. This was such a burden on the tender shoulders, so the wise father bought a small pulled school bag for the child. There has been public outcry every year about reducing the burden of young students. A report says that an electrician carries a 2-kg toolkit; a salesman shoulders a 3-kg backpack; a soldier's rifle weighs 3.7 kg. But a primary schooler's bag can reach 5 kg. Endless home exercises, constant exams, great expectations that parents place on their young, all these weigh heavily on the pulled school bag, an invention that doesn't really help the children realize their dream of a childhood free of worries and troubles.

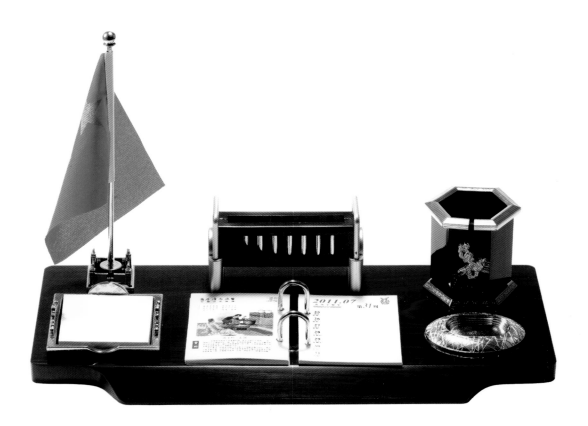

Business calendar

42x26x20cm
Wood, Metal, Fabric, Paper

The calendar might be the most frequently used item on an office desk. The empty space on a calendar is often filled with telephones, appointments and other notes. Before New Year, most stationery and present shops will display various calendars to suit different customers. Many fashion magazines also present a calendar in its last issue of the year. Specially ordered calendars bearing an enterprise's information are ideal gifts that cost little but are seen by the desired customers throughout the year. Designers have added many ingenious devises to the simple calendar. Checking the date is no longer important as compared with added functions such as clock, pen container, calculator, notepad and name card box. Some calendars are decorated with national flags, globe, golden ox and others. Such multi-functionary calendars seem to be quite popular among consumers.

Food & Drink

饮食百味

Erguotou | *Jiaozi* dumpling | Cabbage | Moon cake | Chinese prickly ash | Candied haws on a stick | Preserved egg | Bean curd | Future Cola | Eight Treasures Porridge | Fermented bean curd | Peking chicken roll

Erguotou

12x7x3.5cm
Glass, Aluminum, Wine

Erguotou is a famous liquor made in Beijing. It often appears on tables and effectively gets one drunk quickly. The liquor contained in a small flat bottle of 100 grams is often called "*Xiao Er*" among liquor lovers. The name Erguotou comes from its production technique. The liquor is distilled three times, but the second distillation produces the most mellow and fragrant liquor. With some 800 years of history, Erguotou has been a loyal companion of the common people in Beijing. For foreigners, Erguotou is like a name card of the nation's capital. A singer from Hong Kong once sang that *"a glass of Erguotou chokes one into tears; the roles in Peking Opera deeply attract the audience".* Many hosts use excuses such as "a banquet won't be complete without liquor" or "deep feelings is shown in emptying the glass at a stretch" to persuade guests to down another cup of liquor. Only after five courses and three glasses of liquor are finished does the banquet reach its climax. There are various drinkers' wager games in the country. While ancient scholars composed poems as toasts, modern people usually engage themselves at the finger guessing game. Fortunately, more and more Chinese have learned that persuading their guests to get drunk is not the best or the only way to show their hospitality.

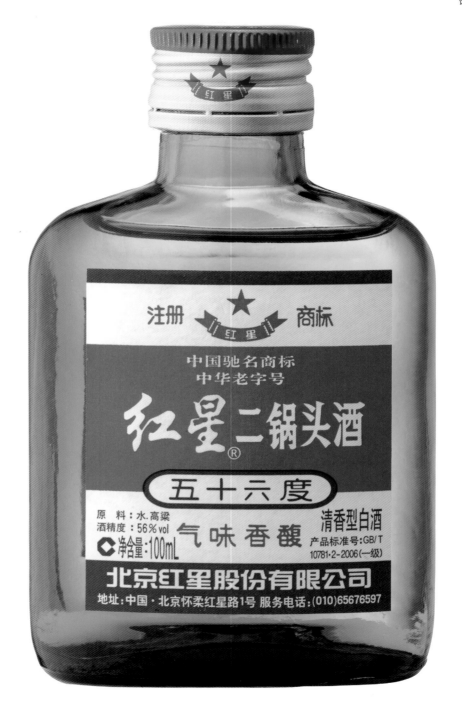

Jiaozi **dumpling**

5.5x3x3cm
Flour, Vegetable, Meat

A popular idiom goes that "no delicacy is better than *jiaozi*, no enjoyment is better than lying down". Eating *jiaozi* dumpling is no big deal today. But a few decades ago, this is a special treat reserved for the year's most important festival – the Spring Festival that marks the beginning of a new year on the lunar calendar. Whether rich or poor, Chinese wouldn't consider the Spring Festival complete or joyful if they didn't make and eat the dumpling. This is especially true in northern China. There are many legends about *jiaozi*. One says that an imperial chef named Wang Xiao'er invented *jiaozi*. But the emperor liked it so much that he wanted to eat *jiaozi* everyday. Wang missed home very much, but he couldn't run away from the imperial palace. On the first day of the lunar New Year, he hanged himself as a protest to the vicious emperor. *Jiaozi* is eaten at midnight to celebrate the arrival of the New Year. In different shapes, *jiaozi* also contains varied fillings. In the past, people would put silver coins, candies or other special things into the dumpling. The one who chanced upon the special filling would be considered lucky. A story says that a student failed to pass the national university entrance examination and didn't want to study any more. On the first day of the New Year, he had *jiaozi* and discovered a special treat upon the first bite. This greatly encouraged him and he eventually entered an ideal university. Years later, he learned that it was his mother who put the special *jiaozi* in his bowl. *Jiaozi* can also be eaten with liquor. It also has many "relatives" such as the wan ton soup and fried *guotie* dumpling.

Cabbage

13x13x22cm
Vegetable

Every winter, the family living at No. 4 in the 5th building of Fuheyuan in Beijing would pile cabbages outside their gate. Storing cabbage for winter is no longer a common practice among Beijing residents. But some families still adhere to the tradition. After the Beginning of Winter which falls in early November, the early snow could ruin all the vegetables in northern China. In the past, each Beijing family would buy hundreds of cabbage to prepare for the wintry season. During the three months or so, most families only saw dishes made of cabbage everyday. Today, advanced agricultural technology and transportation ensure the rich variety on Beijingers' tables in deep winter. Cabbage is no longer a staple. In 2004, Hebei province got a bumper harvest of cabbage. But its price fell to an unprecedented 2 cents per kg. Among the vegetables grown in China, cabbage is very humble – it is fit for all sorts of homely dishes prepared by frying, simmering, being preserved with salt or mixed cold with seasoning. Full of protein, fiber, calcium, phosphorus and vitamins, cabbage is listed as the most reasonable dish in all restaurants. The delicious cabbage fried with vinegar and sugar is easy to prepare and goes very well with rice. Chinese people have special feelings towards cabbage – a common vegetable easy to store and a good companion for the nation through hardships.

Moon cake

4.8x4.8x3.4cm
Flour, Nuts, Egg;
36.3x29.8x6.1cm
Paper

Moon cake is a traditional dessert for the Mid-Autumn Festival that usually takes place in September. Chinese people's love of delicacies is fully displayed here. Mid-Autumn Festival is one of the most important traditional festivals in China. Upon this day, the whole family must stay together under the bright full moon. With fruits and moon cakes offered to the moon, the elders would tell stories of how Lady Chang'e flew to the moon; how the sweet-scented osmanthus tree in the moon can grow again after it is chopped; how the little white rabbit is so lonely up there in the moon. When the stories are told and the incense is burnt, the family would eat the fruits and moon cakes to celebrate the festival. Nowadays, the main dessert for this festival is no longer

intended for the taste buds. Most moon cakes in the market are over-packaged and marked with astounding prices. There was a package of "pure golden Buddha moon cake" that cost 180,000 yuan. Another clever businessman thought of promoting apartments with moon cakes. It is no longer surprising to see moon cakes packed with wine and liquor, dried or fresh fruits, stationery and other presents. The China Chamber of Commerce is drawing "moon cake standards" that give specific requirements on moon cake's packaging. Hopefully, such measures could help moon cake return to its old sweet nature.

Chinese prickly ash

0.4x0.4x0.4cm
Chinese prickly ash

Chinese prickly ash was recorded in *The Book of Songs* compiled some 3,000 years ago. Although this plant can grow in most parts of the country, the Sichuan people are known for their love of Chinese prickly ash. A lot of Sichuan dishes are named with "*ma*" – numb, a physical effect created by Chinese prickly ash on the tongue. At Sichuan restaurants flourishing across the country, one can always delight in a simple dish called *mapo doufu* – a tender bean curd fried with Chinese prickly ash and hot pepper. Besides being an important seasoning for Sichuan cuisine, Chinese prickly ash has also been used in many other ways. Li Shizhen, a renowned doctor of the Ming Dynasty (1368-1644), once cured an old woman of diarrhea with this plant. The strong smell of the dark brown seeds can drive away ants, flies and other insects. In the past, imperial ladies lived in rooms where the walls were paved with Chinese prickly ash. Besides driving away insects, the multi-seeded plant was also seen as auspicious for families anticipating many children.

Candied haws on a stick

4x4x30cm
Haw, Sugar, Bamboo

A few years ago, most TV channels played the same old song: "*Everyone says the candied haws on a stick are sour, but they taste sweet … One such stick can cure you of illness and make you 20 years younger.*" It's an exaggeration but the sweet-sour taste is unique, and there is a story about how candied haws cured a patient. It is said that Concubine Huang, a favorite of Emperor Guangzong of the Song Dynasty (960-1279), once fell ill and didn't want to eat anything. The emperor sought after cures throughout the country. A doctor entered the imperial palace, took the lady's pulse and said she should be fine in half a month, if she ate a few haws simmered with crystal sugar before each meal. He was right, the lady did recover. She probably ate too much greasy food and the candied haws helped her digest. When simmering haws with crystal sugar, it is crucial to regulate the fire. If the fire is too weak, the haws taste sticky; if the fire is too strong, the haws would look dark and taste bitter. Some peddlers put candied haws on a stick and stacked the sticks on a pile of wheat straw. In the old days, peddlers would carry the sticks and call out in a melodious tone to attract customers. In difficult years, eating a stick of candied haws was like celebrating the new year for children. Today, such peddlers are rare and children are often enticed by other attractions.

Preserved egg

5x5x6cm
Egg

Preserved egg, known as *songhua dan* or *pi dan* in Chinese, is a product of chemical experiment. When the duck or goose egg is preserved in a mixture of bittern and the water used in grinding green beans, the protein in the egg subsides and the egg white becomes transparent and greenish. Irregular snowflake patterns dot the egg white, while the yolk becomes juicy and bluish green. The light blue shell makes the egg appear like a fossil just excavated, thus some foreigners call it "thousand-year-old egg". In 2011, preserved egg on top of the most disgusting CNN food. It was described as demon the eggs boiled eggs with weird shape and scary smell. Of course, this comment with strong food preference won't make any negative effect on Chinese continuing likeness to preserved eggs. In any restaurant, you can order the cold dish named preserved egg with bean curd. More flavors can be added with ginger juice or green pepper. Southern Chinese often prepare rice porridge with preserved egg and lean meat. Preserved egg in fish chip soup also tastes excellent.

Bean curd

7.5x5.5x3.6cm
Bean curd

In the 1980s, a story in International Economic Preview published in the United States predicted that in the coming 10 years, it's not the automobiles, televisions or electronic products that will have the greatest market potential, the biggest success belongs to bean curd from China. Obviously, the author is a big fan of bean curd. Although bean curd has not attained such huge success as predicted, it does enjoy equal fame as tea and porcelain from China. It is said that a French artist is fascinated by bean curd. Whenever he feels ill, he would get some bean curd from the China Town in Paris and it never fails him. For most Chinese, the love of bean curd comes from its special taste. Like many inventions that came out of total accidents, bean curd was not invented intentionally. Liu An, a grandson of Liu Bang, founder of the Han Dynasty (206 BC-AD 220), hired many alchemists to make pills of immortality. The Prince of Huainan couldn't escape death, but his experiments brought an unexpected result – bean curd. Liu's hometown, Shouxian county of East China's Anhui province, is known as the Hometown of Bean Curd. Today, any common family in Shouxian can easily cover a table with dishes that all contain bean curd. Bean curd has an amazing adaptability. Each family can easily make the cold dish named bean curd mixed with Chinese onion. The most famous Sichuan dish *mapo doufu* is hot, tender and salty with pepper and Chinese prickly ash. There are hundreds of notable dishes featuring bean curd as the main material. Among Chinese chefs, bean curd is listed as one of four top vegetarian materials. However, many temples have invented bean curd dishes that look and taste just like meat to cater to pilgrims. Such a rich variety makes everyone marvel at the great potentials of bean curd.

Future Cola

26.3x7x7cm
Plastic, Coke

As Coca Cola and Pepsi occupy prominent shelves in department stores across China, most people in rural China only associate cola with a Chinese product named Future Cola. Its Chinese name Feichang Kele means "very enjoyable". In 1998, the Wahaha Group introduced its Future Cola as "real Chinese cola". This won some applause but linking a drink with patriotism has not been a very effective marketing strategy. Soon the advertisements changed into "when happiness arrives, it's Very Enjoyable". It is said that the head of the Wahaha Group once visited the United States and presented guests with two glasses of cola, unnamed. Nobody could tell which was made in China or America. This is only a story, as devoted cola fans can easily distinguish Cola Cola and Pepsi. Although it is hard to find Future Cola in big Chinese cities, Wahaha Group has been promoting another product named Future Coffee Cola. For consumers going after fresh tastes, this has proven rather successful.

Eight Treasures Porridge

12x6.5x6.5cm
Aluminum, Plastic, Porridge

In department stores of China, a common item is Eight Treasures Porridge (*Babao Zhou*). This is actually a simplified version of the *Laba* porridge made on the 8th day of the 12th lunar month. Legends say that Sakyamuni, founder of Buddhism, was enlightened and became Lord Buddha after he was saved by a herdswoman on this day with porridge made of various grains. Many temples would prepare the porridge on this day for pilgrims. Eating porridge at dawn has been seen as an effective way of strengthening one's health. It is not an easy thing to prepare the Eight Treasures Porridge, whose eight chief ingredients vary in different areas. It is true that a bowl of porridge meticulously prepared carries more love than an extravagant banquet. When the canned Eight Treasure Porridge was first introduced, people regarded it as an important present. Thanks to its good taste, the product has held a market share for many years. It would be very appropriate to send a few cans to a patient who can't digest oily food.

Fermented bean curd

12.3x6.8x6.8cm
Glass, Plastic, Bean curd

Just as the idea of fruit wine was inspired by rotten fruits, fermented bean curd (*doufu ru*) probably comes from mouldy bean curd. Since its birth, many people have fallen in love with it. Although most people treat it as a seasoning, some insist that it is good for one's health in prolonging youth, lowering blood fat and preventing Alzheimer's disease. Many places in China are known for the special fermented bean curd they produce. In Guilin of Guangxi Zhuang autonomous region, the fermented bean curd is a good present for friends. In Lankao of Henan province, the fermented bean curd became known throughout the country partly due to Jiao Yulu, a devoted official who died working for the people in the 1960s. The common food seems to contain rich aroma that leaves a deep impression. Zhang Yihe, a writer who talked about her family's life in the 1930s and 40s in Beijing, has a long story about fermented bean curd. From one eatery, she bought five kinds of fermented bean curd made from all across the country. The variety turned the simple breakfast with porridge and steamed bun into a journey of surprising discoveries. An old monk in Zhejiang also eats the same breakfast, but without such variety. Fermented bean curd has become part of his religious life.

Peking chicken roll

20x6x6cm
Flour, Chicken, Vegetable, Sauce

Peking chicken roll has enjoyed great popularity among Chinese customers since Kentucky Fried Chicken invented this delicacy a few years ago. Based on the lotus-leaf pancake eaten with Peking roast duck, it is made by wrapping a thin pancake around fried chicken chips, cucumber, Chinese onion, sweet soy sauce and burger paste. To promote this product, Kentucky Fried Chicken invited Peking Opera actors and actresses to perform in their eateries and required their waitresses to dress like Qing Dynasty maidens. As the world influences China, the Middle Kingdom is also influencing the rest of the world. People want to know more about China. The Great Wall and the Forbidden City are not enough. Details in Chinese people's daily life are getting more attention these days.

At Home
居家市井

Mutton hotpot | Sponge gourd brush | Vegetable scrubber | Small electric oven | Honeycomb briquette |
Gas tank | Thermos | Iron pan | Chopsticks | Candy box shaped like a golden ingot | Glass bottles for tea |
Glue roller | Rolling pin | Thimble | Mandarin duck quilt | Pillow cover | Bamboo mat | Palm-leaf fan |
Lunar almanac | Hot water bottle | Piggy bank | Immersion heater | Clothes scrubbing board | Suction pump |
Scrubbing bath towel | Spittoon | Electric mosquito swatter | Mosquito incense | Motor tricycle taxi |
Mirror | Chinese Lazy Susan table | Red envelope | Spring lock | Cotton Cloth/Plastic Portiere |
Wooden steelyard | Folding stool | Seat Belt Buckle | White Cat Washing-up Liquid | Purple clay teapot |
Dish cover | Bicycle | Mat outside the door | Shower heater | Red-blue-white bag

Mutton hotpot

32.7x32.7x32.7cm
Copper

CHINESE STUFF
中国东西

Mutton hotpot is quite popular with northern Chinese. While ancient Chinese developed many ways to eat with elegance, devouring big chunks of meat was also seen as an enjoyment. The Chinese term for mutton hotpot is *shuan yangrou* – *yangrou* refers to mutton and *shuan* basically means the action of scalding. Legends say that Kublai Khan once led his army to battle. During a break, they boiled water to make mutton soup. But the enemy assaulted them unexpectedly. A chef quickly sliced mutton and threw the chips into the boiling water. He had no time to make a soup, but sent the boiled mutton to Kublai Khan in a hurry. Kublai Khan finished several bowls and felt rejuvenated. He leaped onto the stallion and charged towards the enemy till defeating them once and for all. In old Peking, mutton hotpot must be prepared with high quality red copper pot that is shaped like a miniature chimney with a life buoy on its waist. The charcoal sticks, each measuring 3 to 6 cm, are put horizontally into the bottom of the pot. The smoke comes out of the chimney while the water in the life-buoy-shaped container is boiling. As the diners put mutton slices into the water and stir them till their color changes into light brown, smoke dusts also settle on the diners' hair and clothes. Former Chinese leader Deng Xiaoping once invited former US Secretary of State Henry Kissinger to enjoy mutton hotpot at the famous Donglaishun Restaurant. They probably discussed international affairs after the meal with a smell of smoke and mutton. Back in the 18th century, Emperor Kangxi and his grandson Emperor Qianlong both invited thousands of octogenarians to enormous banquets to celebrate their own longevity in the Forbidden Palace. One of the biggest banquets involved some 1,500 tables featuring mutton hotpot. That could have set a Guinness world record.

Sponge gourd brush

22x7.5x7.5cm
Towel Gourd

As its name suggests, this brush is made from dried sponge gourd. With the skin peeled, the sponge gourd provides tenacious fiber for a brush that is commonly used to clean dishes. As various modern equipment dazzle housewives who fight a continuous battle against dust and grease, few still remember the sponge gourd brush that was born in the agricultural society. Some fashionable people, however, have discovered the miraculous functions of the sponge gourd in clearing away dead skin and encouraging metabolism. In traditional Chinese medicine, the fiber of sponge gourd is often used to tackle inflammation, dissolving swellings and reducing phlegm. In daily life, fresh sponge gourd is an ideal ingredient for soup. It tastes soft, slightly fragrant and melts in the mouth. For the busy urbanites, making a sponge gourd soup can clear away earthly worries and bring back memories in the leisurely countryside.

Vegetable scrubber

27x11.4x2.5cm
Plastic, Metal

It is not clear who invented the vegetable scrubber that, according to peddlers, can turn potatoes, cucumbers and other vegetables into strips, slices and other shapes easily. Chinese pay great attention to the shape, color, smell and taste of each dish. For someone who is not yet to master the dazzling and dangerous skills of cutting and slicing, the vegetable scrubber comes in handy. In *Analects*, Confucius said that no food is made too refined, in other words, there is no boundary in meticulously preparing a meal. The simple vegetable scrubber seems to be a perfect footnote to this ancient maxim.

Small
electric oven

18x18x7.8cm
Metal, Pottery clay, etc.

University students, bachelors, migrant rural workers, they probably share a common tender feeling toward one electric appliance: the small oven. When plugged in, the oven turns hot red in a matter of seconds. Then it's time to prepare a meal. For those who spend much time wandering among world-famous kitchen cupboards for their new apartments, there is absolutely no place for a small oven. But just a decade or so ago, this small appliance was indispensable for anyone aspiring after comfort and joy. The small oven costs less than 10 yuan, easily affordable for most people. It measures only about 20 cm in diameter. One can put it beneath the bed and take it out whenever necessary. The small oven is also cleaner and safer than burning firewood or briquettes. For many people, the portable oven is a mini kitchen that enables one to boil water, cook porridge, dishes, noodles and eat hotpot. Some gourmets even learned to prepare shrimp and crab, simmer oolong or *pu'er* tea with the small oven. The small electric oven has become part of the warm memories of a by-gone era.

Honeycomb briquette

12.2x12.2x8.5cm
Coal

As most Chinese prepare dishes with natural gas sent through pipelines, boil water with liquefied gas contained in metal tanks, make rice with electric cookers and rely on electric heaters in winter, there are some people who are still using honeycomb briquettes. Compared with electricity or natural gas, briquettes are time-consuming, polluting and even dangerous. But this is a cheap source of energy. The global price rise of energy is directly affecting people's lives. When necessary, people wouldn't mind taking the troubles of using the honeycomb briquettes again. A few decades ago, honeycomb briquettes were quite popular throughout the country. Four or five briquettes could keep a small room warm on a wintry day. In those days, it was a steady source of income to send honeycomb briquettes with tricycles into the deep *hutong* lanes in Beijing. Some clever families even took the trouble of getting the raw materials and making briquettes by themselves. In the film *Peacock* directed by Gu Changwei, there is a scene that a sudden downpour reduces the freshly made briquettes into a pile of black dirt. It is full of sadness.

Gas tank

77x30x30cm
Steel, etc.

Using natural gas sent through pipelines is a privilege enjoyed by residents of major cities. In many families, gas tank is still the best thing they can access. When the liquefied gas is about to be finished, an experienced housewife would shake the tank and the remaining gas can boil a bottle of water. It is a labor to carry a gas tank weighing some 20 kg upstairs. For a vigilant mother, an effective way of finding out the capabilities and honesty of her future sonin-law is to send him on a mission of getting a new gas tank. Liu recalls with fondness that in her childhood, her father often carried a gas tank home on the back of his bicycle. In the early 1980s, many buildings were constructed with several families sharing one kitchen and one bathroom. In the small kitchen, each family would have a gas tank and a stove. Ma Junying's family lives in such a building. Each time her husband carries home a new gas tank, she would greet him in her soft voice, while her son would watch his father linking the tank on the stove, turning on the valve and testing the fire. "It works," he would announce and clap his hands, before leading the boy back home to play, while Ma busies with supper. Carrying the gas tank is a very manly job. Before hurdle racer Liu Xiang set a world record and became "Flying Man", his neighbors often saw him carrying gas tanks for the elderly people in the neighborhood.

Thermos

37x15.5x12cm
Aluminum, Glass, etc.

Each Chinese family has one or two thermoses. Even if there is an electric drinker carrying a bottle of pure or mineral water, the elderly people still like to keep the thermoses full of hot water. Not long ago, it was an honor to be granted a thermos printed with colorful patterns and the big character "*jiang*" (award). The thermos was granted if one became a model worker, helped someone in need, or won a prize in a singing contest. Earlier than that, such a colorful thermos with iron surface was a descent dowry. Hai Feng, a traveler, recalls that once he asked for a bottle of buttered tea in a restaurant in Lhasa. The waitress asked him if he wanted a small thermos of 3 pounds, or a bigger one of 5 pounds. Soon, a thermos full of buttered tea was placed in front of him. It was warm until the very last drop. The Chinese are known for the hobby of drinking hot water. But many foreign countries don't follow this tradition. Some Chinese travelers thus take an electric cup that can boil water wherever they go. In Guangdong, where the summer is hot and steaming, desserts stores often put green bean paste mixed with ice in the thermos. This is another wonderful function of the thermos.

Iron pan

44.6x30x9.6cm
Iron, Wood

Almost every Chinese family cooks dishes with a frying iron pan. Despite its humble appearance, iron pan has been proven effective in preventing iron-deficiency anemia. As the fire shines brightly, a light smoke begins to rise from the heated oil. Chopped Chinese onion sizzles in the pan, emitting a fragrance that is prelude to common but delicious dishes. With an iron pan and a spatula, the housewife can turn out various delicacies like a magician. Unlike the Western kitchen that has a specific cooking utensil for each type of food, common Chinese families can deal with frying, stir-frying, steaming, boiling, simmering and other situations with one iron pan. Famous Chinese scholar Hu Shih (1891-1962) liked to treat guests with a dish named Number One Pot. According to another scholar Liang Shih-chiu (1903-1987), the dish was brought to the table in an iron pot with a diameter of more than 60 cm. Above the boiling soup, there are layers of cabbage, turnip, bean curd, pork, duck and chicken dotted with dumpling wrapped in fried egg. "It was very delicious," Liang said. In the 1960s, numerous people joined in a movement to smash the iron pan and other iron utensils in the family to "contribute" to the nation's iron and steel industry. Today, the iron pan can stay safely in the kitchen, fulfilling its simple tasks of cooking. If someone says: "I'll smash and sell my iron pan to...", it is merely a figure of speech that expresses strong will.

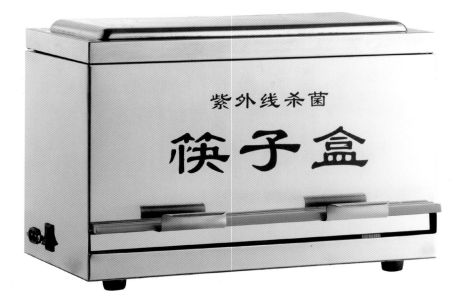

紫外线杀菌

筷子盒

Chopsticks

24x1.5x0.75cm
Plastic;
28x20x17
Iron, etc.

While Chinese often take pride in the rich variety of cuisine across the country, chopsticks have remained the most common tableware in the country. In dexterous hands, the two sticks about 30 cm long can handle everything from fetching a grain of bean to picking out fishbone. For Westerners who grow up with fork and knife, it is a challenge to handle chopsticks upon the first Chinese meal. Opinions differ as to who invented the chopsticks. Popular versions give credit to two men: Da Yu, a legendary man who curbed the floods and became one of the three most famous kings; and Jiang Ziya, a military strategist who helped Ji Fa topple the cruel rule of the Shang Dynasty in the 11th century BC. There are many materials to make chopsticks. Common people use wood and bamboo, while ancient nobles preferred ivory and silver. Plastic chopsticks were once popular in hotels and big restaurants. Disposable chopsticks have become the target of criticism from environmentalists and the whole society. In the land of courtesy, there are many rules about table manners. It is considered very rude to hit the bowl or search for a particular piece in a dish with chopsticks. Planting the chopsticks in a bowl of rice would invite angry glares, as some southern provinces have the tradition of offering rice to the deceased in front of the tomb, with a pair of chopsticks planted in the bowl. In the past, a girl's dowry would always include a pair of chopsticks, as its pronunciation "*kuai zi*" can be expanded to "*kuai sheng gui zi*" – having a son quickly. Emperor Xuanzong of the Tang Dynasty (AD 618-907) once granted a pair of chopsticks to his prime minister Song Jing as a way of praising his outspoken and candid character, because the chopsticks are always straight and unyielding.

Candy box
shaped like
a golden ingot

18.8x10.8x9.5cm
Plastic, Candy

During major holidays such as the Spring Festival, most department stories would promote candy boxes shaped like the golden ingot (*yuan bao*). Looking like a mini shoe, the golden ingot was once a currency in ancient times, but it is more of a symbol of affluence. The plastic candy boxes are decorated like golden ingots and piled together to generate an air of happiness and prosperity. For some families, putting such a candy box in the sitting room is not only a convenient way of treating guests, but also an unspoken invitation to the God of Fortune. Among Chinese friends, it is not common to send a golden ingot candy box as present. But business people do pay much attention to auspicious words and images that they believe could bring blessings. As paper money faces depreciation at any time, the stock of gold has been a country's important economic criterion. There are some people who like to change their money into gold with the hope of guaranteeing its value.

Glass bottles for tea

9x9x22.5cm
Glass, Plastic

Old Huang is a bus driver. He has a huge glass bottle for tea. Everyday before he sets out for work, Old Huang grabs a handful of tea and puts it into the bottle, pours in hot water, tightens the cover and puts the bottle in its special string bag. This is a whole day's drink for Old Huang. At the red light, he would take off the cover and sip the strong tea, enjoying a rare moment of relax in the hard work. Old Huang's bottle used to contain the Nestles coffee. Used bottles for canned fruits and extract of malt and milk powder are never thrown away. Some of the big ones are turned into tea bottles that supply a day's drink. The bottles are made of thick glass that won't crack easily when boiling water is poured in. With a string bag covering the bottle, even hot tea won't burn the hands. Some elderly men in Beijing often take such bottles on their daily routine of playing Chinese chess with old friends under a shady tree, or sing a few arias from Peking Opera. The tea keeps the throat moist throughout the day. As days pass by, the inside of the bottle is covered with a layer of sediment. It is said that sediment from tea does no good to health, hence people have invented many ways to clean it. The most useful methods involve tooth paste or salt. Drinking tea with such big glass bottles has nothing to do with kungfu tea or top grade tea. The most ordinary tea leaves prepared with the common water can bring the folks a day of leisurely enjoyment.

Glue roller

15.5x11x4.5cm
Plastic, Self-adhesive paper

Glue roller is a hand-held gadget with a sticky surface that can clear away threads and dirt on clothes. To solve various problems in daily life, humans have shown great wisdom. In winter, static draws dust, hair and other nuances to the clothes. Some people would take pains picking them off one by one. But ingenious inventors have thought of a better way: taking off the particles with a stronger force than static. The early inventors might have used adhesive tape. It does have a good effect, but it's rather cumbersome in practice. Inspired by the roller that is used to apply paint on walls, someone invented the glue roller which is much easier to use with the handle. When the surface of the roller gets too dusty, one can rip it off without trouble and a new layer of glue is revealed. Besides cleaning clothes, the glue roller is also applied on glass, floor, wall, table, even circuit board. There are thousands of similar inventions that brought convenience to people's lives but haven't established fame for their inventors. For common people, such a small invention is much more meaningful than a nuclear missile that consumes an astronomical sum of investment with the sole aim of mass destruction.

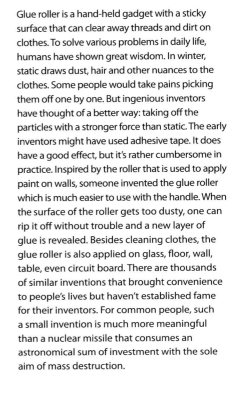

Rolling pin

38x3.2x3.2cm; 25.2x2.6x2.6cm
Wood

Rolling pin is an indispensable instrument for making pasta. When it does make news headlines, the rolling pin is usually a crime weapon used similar to the baseball bat. But that seldom happens and the rolling pin remains a humble member of the kitchen. As the pin rolls back and forth, the dough is flattened, thinned and rounded. In the hands of an adroit mother, the smooth, shiny and chubby rolling pin can work magic. In old times when rice and wheat flour were much coveted scarcities, the rolling pin signaled a big meal. As the mother cleaned the board and pin after making dumplings, noodles or steamed bun, the hungry children would wait around the boiling pot for the great moment.

Thimble

1.8x1.8x1.1cm
Copper

Thimble looks like a ring, but there are many small hollows on its surface. When someone does needlework, he or she can put the thimble on a finger to help push the needle through thick cloth. In the past, young girls would buy a thimble and bring it to the temple, where they would pray for a pair of nimble hands. Whether a girl could make fine needlework was a crucial criterion for her marriage prospects. Not long ago, it was unimaginable that people would throw away old clothes. A big part of a mother's household chores was to make shoes, patch up holes on socks and trousers. All of it was done under the dim kerosene lamp after the rest of the family went to bed. For a diligent mother, the thimble was like a ring that helped her shine in the most difficult times.

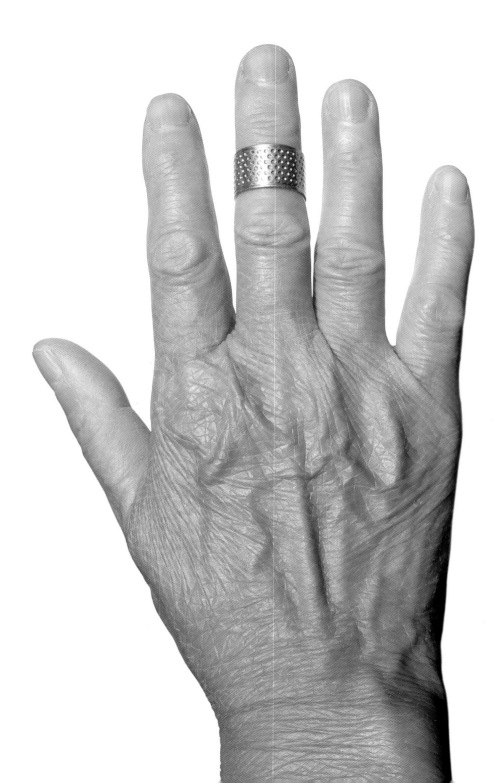

Mandarin duck quilt

56x48x26cm
Cotton, Fabric

In the countryside, quilts with the pattern of mandarin duck are found in almost every family. Upon wedding, the bride's family is responsible for preparing the quilt. A pair of mandarin ducks against red background symbolizes harmonious married life and brings an air of happiness to the wedding chamber. Su Shi, a scholar and poet in the Song Dynasty (960-1279), once wrote a poem describing the marriage of an 80-year-old man with an 18-year-old woman. *"On the night inside the mandarin duck quilt, a tree of white pear flowers stays above the Chinese flowering crab-apple blossoms."* When *Lolita* was introduced to China, some translators used the metaphor of pear flower and Chinese flowering crab-apple to render the film's title. Inside the cover of mandarin duck, most quilts are made of cotton. Over time, cotton becomes tight and it's necessary to make it fluffy again. There is a special cotton-fluffing trade in the country. When there is a family who wants to have its quilts fluffed, the craftsman would pause in his journey and work day and night till all the quilts are fresh and fluffy. Wherever the cotton-fluffing craftsman goes, people always welcome him. A wedding quilt can thus remain fresh for generations. The mandarin ducks are known for staying loyal to one partner for life. The mandarin duck quilt is a very suitable dowry.

Pillow cover

67x47.5x0.3cm
Cotton

If you are invited into a Chinese bedroom, you might notice a towel covering the pillow. The pillow is usually put into a container, but a towel is still deemed necessary as it can be washed more easily. This is one example of how Chinese like to put a cover on anything possible at home. The television, sewing machine and washing machine all have their tailor-made covers. The sofa is always covered on the back and the arms. Even the computers in an office could be protected by a piece of cloth. Some covers carry refined embroidery, making them an interesting decoration to the Chinese home.

Bamboo mat

120x10.8x10.8cm
Bamboo, Vine, Polyester

When young ladies put on slim dresses, summer has arrived. The department stores are the fastest in reaction. They promote various products for the summer. Besides air conditioner and electric fan, the summer sleeping mat always takes up prominent positions. There are various types of sleeping mat made of grass, flax, leather and others. But bamboo mat has been the most popular in the country where bamboo grows in most parts of the land. Bamboo mat has the magical effect of increasing ventilation, absorbing sweat and humid air. It is easy to fold and can be used for many summers. In southern China, people like to spread sleeping mats in the open courtyard during the hottest nights. The chatting and snoring make the summer night an interesting part of Chinese folk life. With a fan and a bamboo mat, Chinese people have spent long summers in the most environmental-friendly manner.

Palm-leaf fan

42x35.3x4cm
Palm-leaf

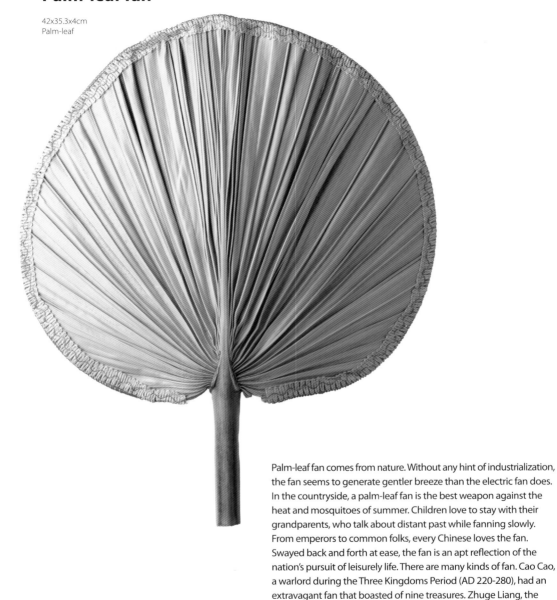

Palm-leaf fan comes from nature. Without any hint of industrialization, the fan seems to generate gentler breeze than the electric fan does. In the countryside, a palm-leaf fan is the best weapon against the heat and mosquitoes of summer. Children love to stay with their grandparents, who talk about distant past while fanning slowly. From emperors to common folks, every Chinese loves the fan. Swayed back and forth at ease, the fan is an apt reflection of the nation's pursuit of leisurely life. There are many kinds of fan. Cao Cao, a warlord during the Three Kingdoms Period (AD 220-280), had an extravagant fan that boasted of nine treasures. Zhuge Liang, the strategist who aided Liu Bei against Cao Cao, always held a fan made of goose feather. Elegant women in the Tang Dynasty (AD 618-907) often half-covered their faces with a round silk fan. The handsome young scholars in the lower reaches of China were known for their folding fans that had calligraphy and paintings. Ji Gong, a legendary monk who helped the poor, carried a broken palm-leaf fan.

Lunar almanac

18.5x12.9x0.2cm
Paper

Lunar almanac (*huang li*, yellow calendar) used to be a guidance for Chinese people's daily life. Most people would check the almanac to see if it was alright for them to do something on a particular day. Even today, the auspicious dates determined by the almanac are still scheduled by most people for their weddings. The yearning for good luck is seen in every aspect of Chinese life. For phone numbers, car license plates and others, Chinese try their best to get "8" or "9", which sound like "prosperous" and "everlasting" in Chinese. When misfortune befalls, some people would consult a geomancer. The lunar almanac is like a geomancer for the common people. It seems to contain everything, from the dates to festivals and the 24 seasonal division points

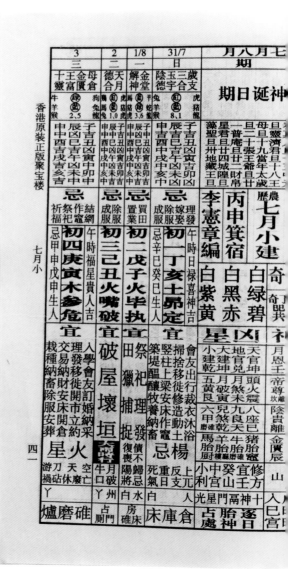

that guided farming practices. It even gives details on lucky or bad directions or hours on a particular day. Few people have inquired into the process of drawing the almanac. Most people just accept everything on the yellowing pages passed down by the generations. It is said that the lunar almanac was created by the legendary Yellow Emperor, that's why it is called the yellow calendar. In feudal China, the almanac was printed officially. The almanac is different year by year. You will come to quite different conclusions if you checked another year's almanac for the same day on the same month. The phrase "old lunar almanac" (*lao huang li*) means to follow traditions strictly without any intention of innovation.

Hot water bottle

27.5x15.7x3cm
Rubber, Tarpaulin

In frigid zones, there are many means to get heat. The hot water bottle might be the most convenient and reasonably priced heating instrument. Made of thick plastic, the flat bottle is soft and one can hold it like a teddy bear. The bottle can hold hot water up to 70°C in temperature and remains warm for several hours. Before the hot water bottle became popular, the elderly people often carried a small container with burning charcoal. The bottle is safer and lighter, winning the hearts of both the old and the young. Traditional Chinese wisdom warns against cold feet. In winter, it is an enjoyment to put a hot water bottle at the feet in bed. With the feet warm, the whole body will feel comfortable throughout the night. Some people have invented a game: blowing air into the hot water bottle. But it is not something that everyone can achieve.

Piggy bank

14.5x11x11cm
Pottery Clay

The chubby pig seems to be an ideal image for gathering fortune. There are legends about fat pigs bringing good fortunes to a family. Some rural women have turned the legends into paper cuts featuring a pig carrying a treasure bowl. For the farmers, the pig is in deed a treasure. As they feed the pigs some leftovers every day, the pigs grow fat gradually. By the last month of the lunar year, the pigs are sold or slaughtered, bringing much needed cash and meat to the family preparing for the important Spring Festival. All piggy banks have only one entrance. To get the coins, one would have to smash it. An ancient Buddhist master once composed a poem that says the piggy bank only wanted to fill its stomach with money, knowing little that in the end, it would be smashed and the money be taken out. But the common people seldom think of the irony behind the piggy bank. For them, saving every penny for a content life is all that matters.

Immersion heater

29.5x4.4x4.4cm
Plastic, Metal

There are dozens of methods to boil water. Electric kettle, electric cup, iron pot, electric rice cooker, water drinking machine and others. Normally, the thermos contains boiled water. But the immersion heater works inside the thermos, together they become a perfect pair. Saving time, water and electricity, the immersion heater is very cheap, costing just a few yuan each. The immersion heater is designed to fit the thermos. The U-shaped metal heater is put into cold water inside the thermos. When it's plugged in, the heater begins working. Some immersion heaters can buzz when the water is boiled. If no one takes care of it, the heater continues working, until the last drop of water is vaporized and a minor fire could be the result. This is the chief shortcoming of the immersion heater, which is why no university allows its students to use this gadget. Because of its cheap price, however, it is still popular.

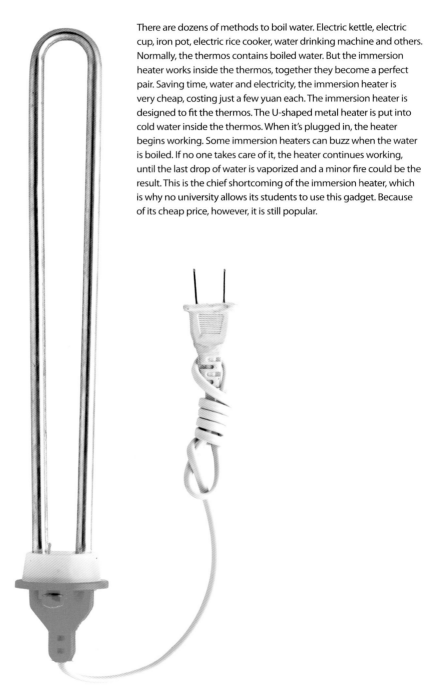

Clothes
scrubbing board

55x16x2.6cm
Wood

Before washing machines became affordable for most families, the scrubbing board was indispensable for each family. The hard-working mothers probably have the deepest attachment to the board, on which they cleaned their children's cloth diapers and the clothes of the whole family. A strong board can be used for decades, until the troughs on its surface are flattened. Tian Dong recently bought a washing machine for his mother. But every morning, the old woman is still washing clothes on the scrubbing board. When the worried son tries to persuade the mother, she says that the washing machine can't clear away all the stains and it wastes both water and electricity. It seems that the scrubbing board is always linked with the mother. A TV ad repeatedly shows an old lady washing clothes on the scrubbing board to promote a washing powder. There is another function about the scrubbing board. When a husband does something wrong, a wife might punish him by ordering him to kneel down on the scrubbing board. Luckily for men, few wives really resort to this last straw. "Kneeling on the scrubbing board" is more of a joke today.

Suction pump

48x13.3x13.3cm
Rubber, Wood

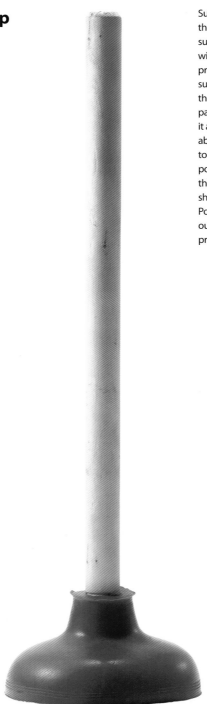

Suction pump is often seen in the toilet. When the sewage system gets stuck, pressing the suction pump on the water exit and pulling it up with force might work. For real tough problems, professional plumbers might charge you a surprising fee. Chinese are often worried about the sewer and many people would put used toilet paper into the wastebasket, instead of flushing it away. Teacher Zhang has worked and lived abroad for many years. He believes discarded toilet paper is smelly and spreads germs. But the potential problems with the sewage system make this a hard choice. There is a *xiangsheng* cross talk show that mentioned the suction pump: "Only the Powerful brand suction pump can pull mankind out of the sea of troubles…" This is a very good promotion for the humble toilet product.

Scrubbing bath towel

20x14x0.5cm
Fabric

When southerners first visit a public bath in northern China, they might be dumfounded by a strange sight: In a spacious hall full of steam, totally naked people stand in the shower, oblivious of other people. In another corner, a group of people chat happily in a huge pool. It is common among northern Chinese to invite their friends to the public bath. Besides bringing shampoo and other stuff, the scrubbing towel is indispensable. With rough surface, the towel is often made like a glove or a square pocket. One can scrub the body to clear away dirt and speed up blood circulation. When you are among close friends, you can ask them to help you scrub the back. It is an intimate moment in a public space. The small scrubbing towel proves to be an effective medium of communication. A few years ago, a Chinese film named *Bath* talked a lot about happenings inside public baths. In southern China, people are used to taking a quick shower once or twice every day. There is no need for the scrubbing towel.

Spittoon

22.8x22.3x22.3cm
Enamel, Iron

For years, Chinese tackled spitting and littering with spittoon. In big families or small homes, a spittoon could be found where the guests would sit. On a photo showing Chairman Mao Zedong and former US Secretary of State Henry Kissinger in Zhongnanhai of Beijing, there is an old style spittoon between them. Some foreigners seem to like the spittoon for its shape, but they do not know its function in China. A former ambassador to China once placed a blue-and-white porcelain spittoon with dried flowers on a long table in the sitting room. The peony flower was once a popular decoration for basin, cup, thermos, spittoon, mirror, quilt, pillow cover and other things. The magnificent flower stood for uniformed aesthetic views in the country. In old lanes of Shanghai, men and women dressed in pajamas could be seen carrying the spittoon to the public toilet early in the morning. For the family members living in a crowded space, the spittoon saved them the trouble of going to the public toilet at night. But as living conditions improve, this is no longer a common scene in the cosmopolitan. With the number of Chinese netizens increasing at an astounding speed, the Internet seems to have become a public spittoon. Many people vent their dissatisfaction or even launch attacks on others under anonymity.

Electric mosquito swatter

50x21.9x4cm
Plastic, Metal

To get rid of mosquitoes, people have invented many methods. The toilet lotion is too gentle, the grass named Chinese mugwort is seldom seen today, the aerosol doesn't seem to work and makes people dizzy, the fly swatter often misses the target. The electric mosquito swatter is based on the fly swatter and looks like a small tennis bat. When the switch is pressed, the metal net is electrified. If a fly or a mosquito touches the swatter, a short circuit occurs and the insect is burned instantly. The swatter is quite safe to use. Even if one touches the metal net, there's no need to worry. On a summer night, it might be a good idea to wander around the house with an electric swatter before going to bed.

Mosquito incense

12x11.5x0.4cm
Propylene Pyrethroid, Wood

The three summer insects – flea, mosquito and fly – are nuisances for every one. Besides causing itchy bumps, the mosquitoes also spread illnesses like malaria and epidemic cerebrospinal meningitis. The mosquito incense is a "chemical weapon" against the annoying insect. As the incense slowly burns, the insecticide is released into the air. The first written record about mosquito incense was made in the Southern Song Dynasty (1127-1279). But it was shaped like a stick. The coiled incense commonly seen today was invented later. Some researchers have found that the coiled incense made of sawdust and rice bran will emit a substance that causes cancer when it is lit. But how to keep the mosquitoes away? There are several suggestions: using mosquito net and window screen to keep them outside your home; put a few boxes of cooling ointment in the room and leave them uncovered; eat garlic, whose smell mosquitoes don't like (your partner probably doesn't, either); dress in white, as mosquitoes favor dark color. Although there are so many options, old-fashioned people still prefer the coiled mosquito incense.

Motor tricycle taxi

215x150x94cm
Metal, Glass, Plastic, Rubber, etc.

Motor tricycle taxis are seen in most cities and towns. The most common type has a canvas-covered seat on the back. Sometimes interesting ads are printed on the canvas that shelters the passenger from sun and rain. The buses can't reach every corner of the city. Taking taxies for a few kilometers is rather costly. Between the bus and the taxi, the tricycles have found their market. In small towns, tricycles seem to be the only means of public transportation. At subway stations or long distance bus stops, tricycle riders often fight for the most advantageous position where they can get the passenger ahead of others. Some cities have banned tricycle taxis for the noise, air pollution and commotion they cause. Still, they are found in the suburbs or the conjuncture of urban and rural areas, sending worn out workers and students to their home at the end of a busy day.

Mirror

18.5x16.5x7.3cm
Plastic, Glass, Aluminum

Archaeological findings prove that as early as the Shang Dynasty some 3,500 years ago, round bronze mirrors had been popular in China. In the Song Dynasty (960-1279), a handle was added to the mirror. It was later improved to be a foldable structure that can keep the mirror erect on the table while the ladies put jewelry into their hair. There are many tales about mirror. It is always linked with the magic power of disclosing the evil spirit's true nature and capturing demons. But in modern China, mirror is nothing special. The plastic mirrors are sometimes decorated with fake diamonds that generate a happy air. Women in the remote mountainous villages still treasure small pocket mirrors that they would take out when no one else is present.

Chinese Lazy Susan Table

180x180x73cm
Wood, Iron, Glass

Chinese Lazy Susan table can usually be found in big Chinese restaurants where people gather together around the table drinking and eating at lunch time or dinner. The Chinese Lazy Susan Table has two parts, the lower part is a fixed table top for placing tableware and the top part is a rotatable glass tray for upon which various dishes are set. Every time you want to eat a certain dish, you need only turn the rotatable tray instead of standing up and make a big fuss. Chinese people not only love to get together in festivals but also like to find some less important reasons for meeting up and having dinner together on regular day. Sitting around square tables is not as harmonious as sitting around a Chinese Lazy Susan table, let alone the limited service for the number of people. Westerners are used to eating alone or at buffets but Chinese are fond of sharing – eating dishes and drinking together at the lively dining table where relationships are strengthened and cooperation develops. The Chinese Lazy Susan table totally fits in Chinese food culture and with Chinese people who love getting together and liveliness. Delightfully, you can get each dish at the table no matter how big the Chinese Lazy Susan table is or where you sit. An person with initiative could turn the rotatable tray by himself and be full (everyone experienced with tourist groups should remember such scene; that eating with other tourists you barely know when the meal time comes and tourist bus stops); a shy person would wait quietly till others turn the table; while a flattering person will turn the table frequently to serve the honorable guest, when this time comes, we are not only eating dishes around the table, but also seeing how relationship turn around.

Red envelope

17x9x0.1cm
Paper

With cash inside, the red envelope is a present on most traditional or modern festive occasions such as someone's birthday, a family moving into a new home, a wedding, a one-month-old newborn's celebration and a student passing the national university entrance examination. While some people seal the red envelope at ease, some do it reluctantly. Lu Xun, a famous writer in the 1930s, once wrote: "People with whom I seldom speak give me a red note printed with 'treacherous hints' such as 'for a sister's wedding' or 'for the wedding of my son', 'we are honored by your presence' or 'we are expecting your grace'. I feel uneasy if I don't spend some money on such occasions. But I don't quite like it." Even though one does not like it, people still get such invitations for various occasions. Bringing red envelope to others' banquets, some people would expect receiving others' red envelopes at their own banquets. This is a red envelope economy in the country. Upon the Spring Festival, the elderly people often give the children red envelopes in the hope of an auspicious new year. But for other times, the exchange of red envelope is done commercially.

CHINESE STUFF
中国东西

Spring lock

10x6.2x2.4cm
Iron, etc.

Spring lock is used in most urban families. In the Chinese dictionary, the definition of "lock" says that it "generally needs a key to be opened". In fact, not all locks need keys. The trick lock, card lock, fingerprint lock and other high tech products don't need keys and they even don't look like traditional locks. The old wisdom that one lock only has one or just a few keys has also lost its charm in modern day technology. The master key can open many locks, a veteran technician can also open a lock with an iron wire. For the common spring lock on the dormitory door, some students prefer using a tough card than the key to open it. To a certain degree, such a lock is more of a decoration, since most people can open it without a key. The ancient Utopian life that "no family closes the door at night, nobody picks up lost things" shall forever remain an ideal. The locks have been developing as the trust on others keeps on reducing. At the low end of the door guardians, the spring lock has so far done a good job.

Cotton Cloth/
Plastic Portiere

240x90x8cm
Cotton;
240x90x3
Plastic, Metal

In the northern part of China, cotton cloth and plastic portieres could be seen everywhere – hanging over dwellings, the stairway and mall entrances, restaurants and all kinds of shops. Plastic portiere are usually used in summer and exchanged for cotton cloth portieres in winter. Portieres are like an unlocked formalistic door that half separates the indoor from the outdoors. It has the spirit of moderatist, neither as isolated as the totally closed door nor as unsafe as the open door. Portieres' purpose is not only for psychological demand of making people feels safe but it is multi-functional. It is convenient for people coming in and out, also for preventing people from the harm of wind, dust, noise, flies, and mosquitoes. At the same time, it prevents

airs made by heating systems or air conditioners from escaping. Each winter, Hongqi street committees would prepare some cotton cloth portieres for "warm the street" activities in which cotton cloth portieres would be hung over doors at buildings, making the indoor as warm as spring. Portieres feel like a vital part of doors for many Chinese and this deepens during a person's life. A lot people are still familiar with the tongue twister named Mian Bu Lian'er: Nan men wai you ge mian pu mian chao nan, mian pu gua le ge lan bu mian bu lian, zhai le lan bu mian bu lian, qiao le qiao, mian pu hai shi mian chong nan, gua shang lan bu mian bu lian, qiao le qiao, mian bu hai shi mian chong nan…

Wooden steelyard

56x50x30
Wood, Iron, etc.

The wooden steelyard is an instrument to measure weight. It is composed of a wooden stick carved with marks, a movable counterpoise on one end and an iron hook with a pan on the other. The wooden steelyard is rarely seen in big cities. But most peddlers still use this instrument in towns and rural fairs. It is said that the wooden steelyard was invented by Laotzu, founder of Taoism who lived some 2,500 years ago. As there are seven stars in the Big Dipper and six in the Southern Dipper, Laotzu decided that 1 *jin* equaled 13 *liang* and put 13 scales, called *xing* (stars), on the wooden stick. The First Emperor of the Qin Dynasty (221-206 BC) added three more scales – the stars of longevity, official rank and good luck – to the steelyard and decreed that 1 *jin* equaled 16 *liang*. The emperor, who united China for the first time in history, ordered businessmen to strictly follow the steelyard and said if they cheated customers by 1 *liang*, they would not gain longevity, high official rank or good luck. The steelyard has been seen as a sign of good luck. When the main beam is installed during the construction of a house, a steelyard is put on the beam in the hope of bringing good luck and prosperity. *Quanheng* is a common Chinese word meaning weighing the gains and losses. *Quan* refers to the counterpoise and *heng* means the wooden stick. Another idiom says "*cheng bu li tuo, gong bu li po*" – the steelyard cannot be without the counterpoise, the husband cannot be without his wife. Only when both man and wife work hard together can they realize a happy life.

Folding stool

28.7x26.8x23cm
Wood, Iron, Fabric

Before the Spring Festival, when tens of thousands of people crowd outside the Beijing Railway Station to begin their journey home for family reunion, the most popular commodity among the passengers is not the Peking roast duck or dried fruits, but the folding stool. Most people are quite happy when they could get a ticket for standing room. If they have a folding stool, that will save them a lot of energy on the crowded train. Ever since the folding stool was invented, it has been used in dramatically different occasions. A housewife sits on it to pick vegetables; elderly people sit on such stools beneath a Chinese scholar tree to talk about history and current affairs, or sip tea and play Chinese chess; young people might bring a stool on a picnic or when they go fishing. The place where you can find the most concentrated folding stools is a military camp. Every soldier is equipped with a green stool. Whether having a meeting or enjoying a film, the soldiers are ordered to put down the stool all at once. Before the film begins, the soldiers often sing, or shout, marching songs. While most people use folding stools that cost a few yuan each, there are some expensive stools made of rare wood by famous craftsmen. Sitting on such a stool, one might feel much more satisfaction and pride, though the hard wooden surface is no more comfortable than common stools.

Seat Belt Buckle

5.6x5x0.5cm
Plastic

Without exception, each car made under global safety standards will have a safety device that will make noisy buzz to remind drivers when they forget to fasten their seat belt. However, for casual and free-spirited Chinese people, many drivers don't want the seat belt to bind their body so they make small tricks by using the seat belt buckle. Where there is demand, there is a market. The seat belt buckle can be searched for online, and have numerous shapes and styles, for instance, buckles with cartoon characters, famous football team logos, motor logos, buckle made of metal, plastic, buckle with crystal and even can be used as a bottle opener. The seat belt inventor Nils Bohlin would be unable either to laugh or to cry if he saw an eyeful of seat belt buckles and for sure he wouldn't understand why those people are so happy without good reason when the price to pay is life. Luo Xiaoming knew the safety performance like the palm of his hand and everything he said about the air bag and the collision avoidance system hit the nail on the head, but he is ever prepared with two seat belt buckles in the car, only because they were free offers when he bought his car.

White Cat Washing-up Liquid

24.5x5.5x5.5cm
Plastic, Surfactant, etc.

Washing-up Liquid, just as its name implies, is a cleanser that is used to wash up dishes, vegetables and fruits. It is a necessity for each family. In the past few years when domestically made products became popular again, fashionable young people switched their attention from the famous Feiyue Shoes and Meihua Sports clothes to every domestically produced industrial product that was symbol of the time. At the same time, they are proud of using domestically produced products which are considered fashionable. Someone painted the White Cat Washing-up Liquid bottle into T-shirts as an individualized decoration, echoing from a distance the artistic thoughts of Andy Warhols Campbell's Soup. The high quality and inexpensive White Cat Washing-up Liquid is a typical domestic product which has been popular for half a century all over China. White Cat Company didn't know it's popularity initially, perhaps its fame has something to do with Comrade Deng Xiaoping's quotes "It doesn't matter if a cat is black or white, so long as it catches mice". This quote on cat has run through each phrase and social rank and became a guide to action for a whole age when people's thoughts were very active and they believed that economic development was the top priority. This coincidence added vitality to White Cat Washing-up Liquid, and it at least occupies a certain place in people's hearts, be they housewives or fashionable youths.

Purple clay teapot

12x8x6.5cm
Violet Sand

The purple clay teapot (*zisha hu*) is a special product of Yixing, East China's Jiangsu province. Locals claim that only the "earth of affluence" found in Yixing can make top quality teapot. Most teapots are shaped simple but elegant. The wonderful thing with the purple clay teapot is that purple clay can keep the tea warm and fragrant for a long time. The older a purple clay teapot, the silkier its surface becomes and the more fragrant the tea is. Chinese people have a long history of cultivating and making tea. There are many books about every detail of enjoying tea. Quite a number of famous ancient scholars have discussed teapots and the purple clay was their favorite. Mei Yaochen, a poet in the Northern Song Dynasty (960-1127), wrote about preparing tea with the purple clay teapot: "*The cold stream by the small rocks maintains the fresh taste, the newly made purple clay brings spring blossoms.*" In the Ming Dynasty (1368-1644), there was a kind of purple clay teapot called *gongchun hu* (supplying spring teapot), but no such teapot is preserved until today. Shi Dabin, Li Zhongfen and Xu Youquan were three most famous craftsmen making purple clay teapots in the Ming Dynasty. Each teapot they made were treasured and honored. In the modern society, more and more people rediscover the joy of appreciating tea. In tourism regions and antiques markets, you can find many purple clay teapots. But it's hard to find real good products from Yixing. If at the depth of night, one could prepare fresh tea with a top quality purple clay teapot and sip from a purple clay tea cup, what more could he aspire after?

Dish cover

45x45x30cm
Metal, Gauze

The dish cover is inspired by the umbrella. When folded, it takes little space. Fully opened, the cover looks like an umbrella that shelters the dishes from insects. Many Chinese families kept unfinished dishes on the table before refrigerators became popular. The gauze on the cover keeps air ventilating while insects can't get a bite of the dishes. Made of bamboo strips, Chinese sorghum branches, plastic and even metal, the dish cover is often decorated with a lace rim, adding a bit of romance to the table.

Bicycle

180x107x60cm
Metal, Rubber, Plastic, etc.

Bicycle isn't a Chinese invention, but Chinese bicycles often have a basket in the front and a child's seat at the back. For decades, hordes of bicycles stream along cars during rush hour, turning the country into a "kingdom of bicycles". In the 1960s and 70s, bicycle, sewing machine and wrist watch were the three major assets of a common family. If someone lost a bicycle, the public security bureau would handle the case with great force. Today, common bicycles represent the common people's social status. They carry the duties of sending children to school and getting vegetables on the way home. Often, it's the grandpa who carries the child, as the parents are busy working in the massive city and school buses are not yet common in China. Parents are invariably concerned about their only child's safety. Very few families would allow their juniors to go to school by themselves. As more parents send their children to school, more traffic congestion is caused near the kindergartens and schools. Then the parents are increasingly worried about their children. This has become a vicious cycle. China Central Television's news magazine *Oriental Horizon* once did a program that shows 85 percent of the surveyed people have been escorting their children between home and school, 83 percent of the parents say their work has been affected. Just like bicycle is a name card for the country, sending children to school has also become a social phenomenon.

Mat outside the door

59x38x1cm
Plastic

To keep the home clean, almost every family has a mat outside the door, so family members and visitors can wipe their shoes before entering the door. Some people say 90 percent of the dust inside a house is brought in by the shoes. On the rainy or snowy days, the mat does an especially good job in keeping most of the mud beneath the shoes off door. The mat can be made of plaited or woven rushes, straw, hemp, or some other pliant material. Red plastic mats in hotels and restaurants are often printed with "welcome" or "safety coming and going". Since the mat became popular, it has become part of the etiquettes to wipe one's shoes on the mat before entering the door.

Shower heater

36.5x36.5x20.6cm
Metal, Glass, etc.

Since shower heater was introduced to China, it has gained great popularity and many enterprises have added more functions to it. With infrared lights and a fan, the heater can quickly raise the bathroom's temperature, pump out humid air, providing lighting and even physiotherapy. To the south of the Yangtze River, the cities don't have public heating system. It takes great courage to expose oneself in the frigid air for a shower. In northern China, where most residential areas are provided with centralized heating system, it's still not warm enough to ensure a comfortable bath. In the past, Chinese would go to public baths once every week or even longer. As people's living conditions improve, taking shower in one's own toilet is an easily accessible enjoyment. But the apartment's heating system was installed years ago. The bathroom heater is a worthy investment to tackle this problem.

Red-blue-white bag

75.5x36x14.5cm
Plastic

The plastic bag with red, blue and white stripes is used widely in China. The plastic is originally a cover for construction sites. Many people call the bag "snakeskin" because of its coloring and rough surface. The big bag can contain a quilt and many sets of clothes. It is stronger than common plastic and protects items inside when a family moves to another house. Many migrant workers carry such bags, which are very cheap. An old man named Wang Wanlin has been helping waifs in Hangzhou of Zhejiang province. The old man has no children himself, but the 400 children he helped all regard him as Dad or Grandpa. His biggest fortune is a red-blue-

white bag containing some 1,000 letters from his "children". This might be the most touching content such bags carry in the world. In 2007, Louis Vuitton introduced a new smaller bag with exactly the same red, blue and white pattern. Even though "Louis Vuitton" is printed on the bag, Chinese consumers can hardly associate it with the world-famous luxury brand. People are surprised at the minute difference between the common and the fashionable. Hopefully, the common bags won't become expensive thanks to Louis Vuitton.

Leisurely Recreation

玩乐闲趣

Popgun | Glass ball | Disposable cigarette lighter | Chunghwa cigarette | Mahjong | Shuttlecock | Grasshopper cage | Huarongdao puzzle | Military chess | The Shenzhou Spaceship Model | Sandbag | Cloth tiger | Radio | Ornamental walnut

Popgun

102x15x5
Plastic, Metal

The "bullet" used in the popgun is actually a kind of needle. Many Chinese would remember that on the busy street, a peddler would erect a piece of cloth studded with balloons. A few meters away, he puts a popgun on a wooden frame. If someone hits a balloon, the peddler would grant the winner a small award, or allow him or her to play again free of charge. The popgun doesn't have a very high accuracy. It takes the shooter some time to find the best angle. Such a game is often played in counties or small towns, like the place depicted in the film *Xiao Wu* directed by Jia Zhangke. Several young people wander in town, they find the popgun and spend a few yuan to shoot the balloons, venting their excessive juvenile energy. Ye Xing left his rural home in Jiangxi province to work in Wenzhou of Fujian. In his spare time, the young man often plays the popgun. With a cigarette at the corner of his mouth, Ye narrows his eyes and zooms in on the balloons waving in the wind. In a loud crack, a balloon disappears. The peddler remains expressionless. A few sparrows take flight.

Glass ball

1.4x1.4x1.4cm
Glass

Before Playstation or Nintendo grabbed children's attention, young boys and girls had many creative games. While girls played with rubber band, boys would lie on the ground on their stomach, focusing on the glass balls. There are many types of glass balls. Some has three leaves of different colors inside; some has three leaves with the same color; some are totally transparent with nothing inside; some has a rough surface; some milky white balls are painted colorful on the surface, which are always vied and treasured by the children. Playing glass balls was quite popular in the 1980s. There were different game rules, but they all brought the children endless joy. One has to be careful with the angle and strength of hitting the ball, which makes the child's game quite similar to snooker. Few children still enjoy the freedom of lying on the ground to play the glass balls. There is too much homework and the parents hate to see their children getting so dirty. The most convenient place to find glass balls is the Chinese chequers, a game that involves groups of balls in different colors.

Disposable cigarette lighter

7.5x2.2x0.9cm
Plastic, Metal, Butane

The disposable cigarette lighter that can't be refueled is rather cheap. From getting fire through drilling on the wood till inventing gunpowder, Chinese have always had their own views on fire. The cigarette lighters can be bought on every roadside cigarette stand at just 1 yuan. If the lighter is kept burning for a long time, it may explode. Once there was a taxi that caught fire suddenly. Firefighters found out that the driver left a disposable cigarette lighter under sunlight for a long time before it exploded and caused the fire. Some times, you don't need to buy the cigarette lighter. Before smoking was banned in public places, some restaurants liked to offer cigarette lighters with their names to smokers. Some beer producers also favor cigarette lighters as a cost-effective advertisement, believing that most drinkers in the country are also smokers. It is reasonable that the cigarette stores would offer a lighter with each pack of cigarettes sold. The disposable cigarette lighter is also an important export item. When the European Union launched an investigation on the dumping of Chinese cigarette lighters, businessmen from Wenzhou of Zhejiang province traveled to Europe, trying to uphold the rights of the small cigarette lighters.

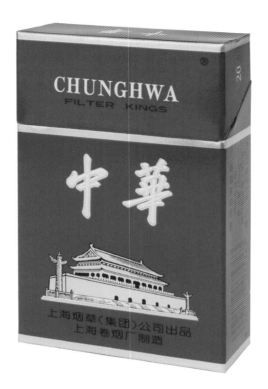

Chunghwa cigarette

9x5.5x2.1cm
Paper, Tobacco

Chunghwa (China) is the most important cigarette in China. Its pack is printed with the Chinese red. Among the numerous cigarettes produced in the vast country, Chunghwa is the only one that can be called a "national cigarette". After the People's Republic of China was born on Oct 1, 1949, the State-owned Chunghwa Tobacco Company in Shanghai undertook the task of producing "the best cigarette". When the first Chunghwa cigarettes were sent to Beijing, Chairman Mao Zedong and other central leaders were very satisfied. Their support helped Chunghwa to gain green light from research to development, raw material supply and mass production. When it was first introduced to the market, Chunghwa quickly replaced an old brand named Baixibao to become the top-selling cigarette. The birth of Chunghwa cigarette was the fruit of a political mission. Even today, while Chunghwa enjoys great popularity in the country, it is still political. When high quality tobacco leaves were in short supply, the State Council issued a letter to tobacco production regions, asking them to send top quality leaves to Shanghai, so the Chunghwa cigarette could be produced smoothly. The cigarette is always prepared on national banquets, Chinese leaders also like to present it to foreign dignitaries. With such fame, Chunghwa is rather expensive compared with other local brands. People in the official circle all like to smoke Chunghwa and claim that they bought the cigarette by themselves.

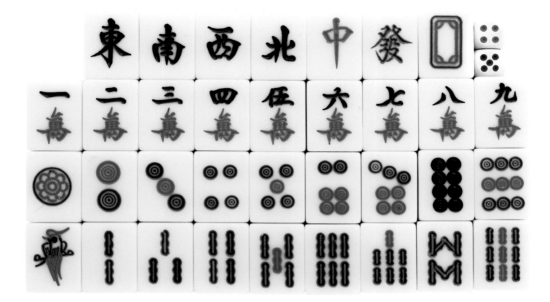

Mahjong

26.6x22.3x5.3cm
Plastic

Mahjong is one of the most popular games in China. Four people play a total of 136 pieces. Some people joke that mahjong is the fifth invention of the country. In terms of recreational influence, no other game can compare with mahjong. Mahjong is also nicknamed "*ma que*" (sparrow) and mahjong players are called "*que you*" (sparrow friends). It has a long history and basic rules were settled as early as the mid-Qing Dynasty (1616-1911). Liang Shih-chiu once said that "where there are Chinese, there is mahjong". Liang Qichao, who aided Emperor Guangxu in political and economic reforms at the turn of the 20th century, was a super mahjong fan. Many of his commentaries were composed over the mahjong table. Many mahjong players like to quote Liang's saying "only when reading can I forget mahjong, only when playing mahjong can I forget reading". In the 1820s, mahjong was introduced abroad and won many fans. Hu Shih wrote in his short article *Mahjong* that "nobody has dreamed that the pioneers in the Oriental culture's Western excursion were the 136 mahjong generals". For some people, mahjong has become the sole means of recreation. Over the Spring Festival, most families would stay by the television for the evening gala show on China Central Television. Both young and old would play mahjong to spend the long holiday. It is unreasonable to require everyone to be ambitious, and it is unnecessary to regard mahjong as a monster that swallows time and money. The game does help many elderly people spend the last years of their lives happily. At the funeral of her grandma, a girl placed mahjong pieces in an order that would win the highest amount of chips in a game. One's character is reflected faithfully in the way he or she plays mahjong. A quiet person might remain composed at losing or gaining huge sums, an impetuous person might upset the whole table at the smallest errors.

Shuttlecock

22x12x10cm
Feather, Plastic, Metal

Kicking the shuttlecock is a traditional folk sport in China. The shuttlecock is made with feather, thread or paper. From young children to old people, almost everyone can enjoy the game. The bricks carved with images in Han Dynasty (206 BC-AD 220) tombs show people kicking the shuttlecock. The game has been popular since ancient times, which is not surprising. Some ancient records describe the game as interesting and elegant as "admiring flying butterflies or a nimble swallow, picking lotus roots, searching for Chinese *mei* blossom in snow". The shuttlecock is easy to make and play. Both the players and the audience enjoy the game. In parks and squares across the country, there are shuttlecock kickers almost every morning and dusk. There is no international match for the game yet. But its influence on common Chinese is comparable with Olympian games. Playing the shuttlecock demands more skill than strength, which is just like table tennis, badminton, gymnastics and diving. Chinese people usually excel in such sports. Saving a shuttlecock that is about to fall on the ground with a dashing pose can bring the same pleasure as winning an Olympic game.

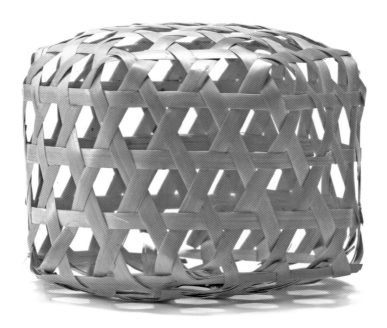

Grasshopper cage

7.5x7.5x5.5cm
Bamboo

Grasshopper is a singing insect favored by many Chinese. The male grasshopper can play musical chirping with its wings. Many people mistake cricket for grasshopper. Actually, grasshoppers are tireless singers, while crickets are more like fighters. Every summer, peddlers carrying hundreds of grasshopper cages would wander along the street. Unlike other peddlers that have to call out in various ways to gain attention, the grasshopper seller employs hundreds of singers. Together with its cage made of sorghum branch, the grasshopper is usually sold for just a few yuan. People like to put the cage on the balcony, hoping that the chirping would bring an air of the summer field. Among the pets, grasshopper is easier to keep. Though it lives for just a few months, the grasshopper is content with cabbage leaves and beans. Keeping the grasshopper and cricket used to be a privilege among the rich and noble families. In the early 1950s, it was criticized as a decadent way of feudal life. Keeping grasshopper enjoys more followers today. The fans are not satisfied with the sorghum cages and make better ones with bottle gourd, bamboo, iron, silver, copper, even jadeite. The delicate and refined cages can be home for thousands of grasshoppers until they become cultural relics.

Huarongdao puzzle

14.3x12x1.4cm
Wood

Huarongdao is a famous sliding block puzzle combining math with a story from the Three Kingdoms Period (AD 220-280). Together with Rubic's cube and diamond puzzle, they are called "three unimaginable puzzles of the world". Huarongdao, Seven-Piece Puzzle (*Qiqiaoban*) and Nine Connected Rings (*Jiulianhuan*) are three most famous traditional Chinese puzzles. In history, Cao Cao lost the war at Chibi (Red Cliff) against Sun Quan and Liu Bei. He pulled back in a hurry, but Guan Yu, Liu Bei's sworn-in brother, ambushed Cao Cao at Huarongdao. Before taking an order from Zhuge Liang, the strategist aiding Liu Bei, to ambush Cao Cao, Guan pledged that if he didn't succeed he would be willing to die. But before the war, Cao Cao had been very kind to Guan Yu. The general just couldn't kill the man who once helped him. Learning that Guan Yu let Cao Cao loose, Zhuge Liang threatened to kill him. But Liu Bei pleaded for his brother and Guan was saved. In front of human relations, rules and laws became flexible. The puzzle has 10 pieces on a board with 20 squares. The pieces of varying size are printed with the faces of Cao Cao, Guan Yu, Zhang Fei and Zhao Yun (both are Liu Bei's sworn-in brothers), two other generals Ma Chao and Huang Zhong, as well as four soldiers. There are only two empty small squares. Those who can get Cao Cao to the exit with the least moves win the game. There are many fans of this puzzle. A math professor named Xu Chunfang has found a solution that involves 100 steps. Jiang Changying, a scientist, has initiated the Huanrongdao Society that focuses on reducing the steps of solving this puzzle.

Military chess

34x24x0.9cm
Plastic

The military chess has been a favorite recreation among Chinese for decades. Not everyone has the chance to go to the battlefield, but almost every boy is deeply fascinated by the military chess. A boy becomes a general when directing the 25 pieces to battle. The early military chess had two opponents. Later two more were added. This made the game rather complicated as the different sides have to seek alliance and fight the enemy with great tactics. The four-kingdom military chess is a much acclaimed game online. It is said that hundreds of thousands of people join the battle everyday.

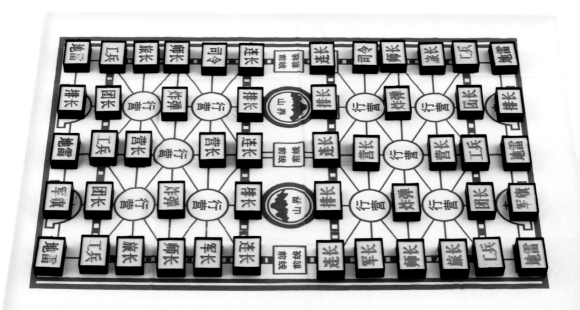

The Shenzhou Spaceship Model

31.5x35x10cm
Metal, Wood, etc.

Early on the morning of the 16th October, 2003, Yang Liwei stepped out of the Spaceship, and the Shenzhou Spaceship Model became the most adored chidlren's plaything and many chose astronaut as an ideal career choice. As the first Chinese person who went to outer space, Yang Liwei is the national hero of China without doubt and he represents the height of China. In September 2008, after a successful Olympic games in Beijing, Zhai Zhigang walked in outer space and realized the flying dream of the Chinese people. From the Shenzhou-1 in 1999 to Shenzhou-7 in 2008, Chinese went to outer space seven times and our feeling about the sky changed subtly. We are now able to touch the nothingness of the vast sky and overlook our home planet. It was interesting to review things that were carried into the spaceship, a national flag, an Olympic flag, Chinese currency, paintings, drawings by kids with outer space themes, and various crops seeds, even the logo of Jinlilai… perhaps each thing was chosen wisely and contained a certain meaning. For most people, outer space is still an unreachable dream even if one day there is outer space tourism. However, at least we are able to see our fellow countryman flying into the sky, walking out of the spaceship and appreciate it as a personal favor.

Sandbag

8x7.5x6cm
Fabric, Sand

Fist-sized sandbag is made of cloth and filled with sand, rice or bean. Compared with "Dropping and Finding Handkerchief", a gentle game in kindergartens, throwing sandbag is almost like a war. Two groups of people take turns to throw the sandbag. The one who is hit is off the ground. But if he or she can catch the sandbag, a precious point is earned. For boisterous children, this is an ideal game that allows them to shout and run. During the 10-minute break at school, the students can manage a few rounds on the narrow corridor outside the classroom. Even if the teacher scolds them for being naughty, the children won't give up the fun. The really good sandbag players have the potential of becoming good soldiers or softball players. Some residents in Fengtai district of Beijing invented the sandbag softball and it was very popular even among adults. Assaulted by numerous new toys and heavy homework, today's children seldom have the time to discover the fun of playing sandbags. It is a precious memory for many adults.

Cloth tiger

14x10.5x10.5cm
Fabric, Cotton

The traditional festivals offer adroit mothers many chances to give their children some surprise gifts. The Duanwu Festival which falls on the 5th day of the 5th lunar month is a commemoration for ancient patriotic poet Qu Yuan. Besides eating the pyramid-shaped *zongzi*, some regions in the country have the tradition of giving children cloth tigers. The 5th lunar month is seen as a time when insects and plagues appear. Making cloth tigers for children is an expression of the wish that the children would be strong as tigers. The mothers make all sorts of things associated with tiger: tiger toys with one, two or four heads; pillows with tiger head, hats and shoes with tiger. There are various types of tiger. But most of them have a big head. An old saying goes that "a 10-*jin* (5 kg) tiger has a 9-*jin* head". The tigers all have a black character "*wang*" (king) embroidered on the forehead, since tiger is seen as the king of all animals in the country. But for today's children, maybe the chubby Japanese cartoon cat Doraemon has more appeal than the traditional Chinese tiger.

Radio

13x8x3cm
Plastic, Metal, PCB, etc.

Radio is no longer an important tool for people to enjoy life. A radio is no longer indispensible for one to listen to radio programs, as the mobile phone, the MP3, even the digital camera, can receive radio waves. Back in the 1980s, a young man would be very proud if he had a radio. Before television became the ruler of a family's sitting room, radio was a prominent and valuable appliance. It used to be a common way of life for a whole family to gather by the radio for news and storytelling programs. Until today, many people still turn on the radio at 6:30 am for *News and Newspaper Clippings* on Central People's Radio. This is an old habit just like watching the *News Relay* on China Central Television at 7 pm. The many frequencies all have certain music programs that invite listeners to interact with the host/hostess. It was quite popular to order a song for someone special. If a daughter ordered a song for her mother on the radio, the mother would probably be moved to tears. *Blessings*, a song by Hong Kong pop star Jacky Cheung, was one of the most frequented ordered songs on radio. Today, a common radio can play dozens of channels. But there are far less listeners, most of whom are the elderly people and migrant workers. The elderly carry a small radio while walking in the park, and the migrant workers listen to pop music to kill the long nights.

Ornamental walnut

4.3x3.5x3cm
Walnut

Many old men like to juggle a pair of big walnuts in their palm. It is similar to rotating a pair of steel balls either clockwise or anticlockwise with one hand. Master An has been playing the pair of walnuts for five years. He says they have become part of him. If he put them down, he would feel very uncomfortable. As he turns the walnuts around, Master An chats with an old man sitting under a tree with his bird cage, then watches some chess players inside a *hutong* lane. The walnuts look smooth and translucent as he plays them almost at every waking minute. A big fan of walnut can talk about it for hours. Walnuts are highly nutritional and decorative. There are cheap ones sold for just a few yuan per pair, but there are also highly prized pairs that can fetch thousands. For centuries, ancient collectors have vied for top quality walnuts. Researchers have found that playing walnuts does help quicken blood circulation and improve one's health.

Attire
穿戴衣着

Safety helmet | Quick tie | Gauze mask | Red scarf | Red sleeve badge | Red cordon | Shoe-pad |
Red underwear | Sun Hat with Face Cover | Split pants | Three-lines badge | Liberation Shoes | Hotel slippers

Safety helmet

26.2x23x17cm
FRP, Plastic

There are many safety helmets such as those for police, motorbike drivers and cyclists. A common safety helmet seen in the city is an indispensable protection for construction workers. Made of plastic, aluminum or glass-fiber reinforced plastic and other materials, the helmets have various functions. Some helmets can reflect the weakest light at night, some fends off the cold in winter, some quickly sends humid air away. The safety helmet used to be a symbol of the working class. Today, it is often associated with migrant workers. A miner named Nie Wenqing was buried underground for dozens of hours before he was salvaged. In despair, he wrote his will on the helmet. The safety helmet cannot prevent all disasters, but it does bring a sense of safety. Nowhere in the world can be called totally safe. While gaining freedom, modern people also lose the sense of safety. S.H.E, a pop band, sings that *"if you don't feel safe, fasten your seat belt; if you don't feel safe, put on your helmet"*.

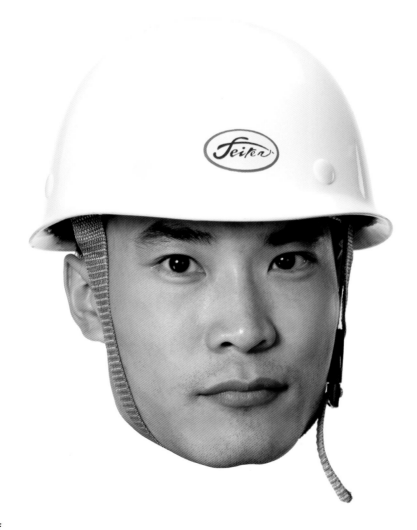

Quick tie

63.5x9x2cm
Fabric

Traditional Chinese dress doesn't need the tie. But Western dressing code has become popular in the country. While learning from other cultures, Chinese are versatile in adaptation. The tie has proved to be rather complicated and time-consuming. Hence someone invented the quick tie (*yi la de*) – a tie with a zip. Looking like a tie, the quick tie is thin and rigid, like the fast foods in a consumer society. Modern people have an unreasonable craze after speed. The fast-frozen *jiaozi* dumpling, tea bags, instant coffee, automatic camera, disposable underwear, all of them are invented to save time. Actually, using the quick tie every morning saves only a few minutes. But it bespeaks of a lack of respect for the quality of life – quietude, leisure and ample time to savor everything.

Gauze mask

31x11x0.3cm
Cotton, Gauze

Due to the strong wind that brings much dust and sand, women in northern China have to put a transparent scarf around their head as they ride the bike between work and home. Inside the scarf, they have another layer of protection: the gauze mask, which is commonly worn by surgeons. The gauze mask can keep dust away from the nose and mouth, also keeping a safety distance between a patient and others. For years, the gauze mask was used mainly in medical services and food industry. In the spring of 2003, gauze mask became an indispensable weapon for almost everyone. Due to SARS, the air in Hong Kong, Guangzhou and Beijing became almost terrifying. To fight against an enemy that they can't see, the common people kept washing hands and wearing the gauze mask when they had to leave home. On the streets, in buses, department stores and elevators, white gauze masks were seen everywhere. When Hong Kong pop star Leslie Cheung (Zhang Guorong) committed suicide, fans and other stars had to wear the gauze mask to attend his funeral. That spring seemed long, but eventually it passed. Humans have angered nature in many ways, SARS is just one of the warnings that mankind should learn to behave themselves.

Red scarf

77.5x29x0.1cm
Fabric

The red scarf is a symbol of the Young Pioneers. An introduction from the former Soviet Union, the red scarf is revolutionary in essence. All primary students who get a better than average score in study can join the Young Pioneers. At the ceremony, a senior Young Pioneer would help the young to put on the red scarf. The teacher would talk about the glorious tradition of the red scarf, which is a corner of the red flag. Its color symbolizes the blood of numerous revolutionists who gave up their lives for the founding of New China. Many people still remember that teachers would scold those who forgot to put on the red scarf in the morning. When the students gather on the playground for morning exercises, the teachers would check if anyone has forgotten the red scarf. A worker recalls that when he joined the Young Pioneers, he would wear the red scarf even in bed. "I wouldn't take it off, which made me a laughing stock," he says. Jiang Hanyu, 61, had the honor of seeing Chairman Mao Zedong. He took off his red scarf and tied it on the neck of New China's founder.

Red sleeve badge

22x14.5x0.1cm
Fabric

Put on the arms, the red sleeve badge used to be a symbol of role model and power in revolutionary years. Today, the badge doesn't carry much ideological color, but plays functions in managing the traffic. In the 1990s, Old Wei worked in the security department of a governmental agency. He was later assigned the job of "traffic assistant", helping the police keeping traffic order on the crossroad. The red sleeve badge is also worn by elderly ladies and men who are assigned the task of keeping an eye on anything abnormal by the neighborhood committee, a grassroots administration appointed by the government. In recent years, people who have bought apartments from the market, instead of being given a dormitory by their units, often complain about the real estate managers. Some of them have put on red sleeve badges and gathered to protest. The loveliest red sleeve badge is worn by young students who take turns to clean the classroom or keep order on campus. In a restaurant in Guangdong, the staff all wear green military uniforms and red sleeve badges. This is a special way to attract old customers who are reminiscent of the revolutionary years and younger guests who are curious of anything different.

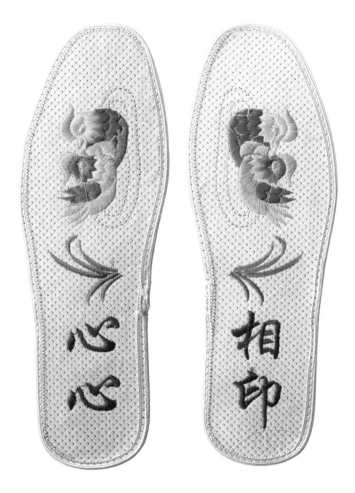

Shoe-pad

27x10x0.3cmx2
Fabric

Shoe-pad is often neglected when people choose new shoes. Actually, a pair of good pads can absorb sweat, prevent odor and bring comfort. Some smart businessmen have discovered the value of shoe-pads. Zhang Hong, a woman in Wanzhou of Chongqing, put fashion elements into the ancient embroidered shoe-pads. For merchants, she promotes a series called "instant success"; for public servants, she designed "continuous promotion" series; for drivers, "safety drive"; for lovers, "mandarin ducks playing on water" (an old symbol of everlasting love). No wonder her business has been prosperous. In supermarkets and on roadside stalls, there are just a few types of shoe-pads available. The disposable mass-produced pads are sold for just 1 yuan per pair. In the past, mothers would make embroidered shoe-pads for the whole family. Every year, Xiao Mei's mother would make a pair of comfortable shoe-pads for her. Upon her wedding, she got two pairs. One pair was embroidered with the words "*qinqing*" (affection), the other, "*aiqing*" (love). Such shoe-pads mean much more than their functional purpose and carry good wishes from a loving mother. Not every woman is good at needlework, but every mother is willing to devote herself to the children. The hand-made shoe-pads provide silent protection to the children.

Red cordon

100x17x0.2cm
Fabric

Chinese are proud of their ancient civilization and pay special attention to greetings. Some people believe that the more complicated the reception, the more respect they show to the honored guests. At many tourist regions, there are employees working as guards of honor, who are dressed in ancient costumes and perform reception ceremonies as recorded in history. Not everyone has the opportunity to attend a State-level ceremony for foreign dignitaries. But chances are you can find a pair of young ladies dressed with a red cordon standing on both sides of the gate at exhibitions, department stores, restaurants, companies and other places. Wearing a smile, the ladies would bow to guests, saying: "Welcome" or "Thank you". This can make a guest feel rather special. Most of the red cordons are made of a layer of red cloth which is covered by a strip of satin. The yellow words are printed onto the satin instead of being embroidered. Some higher quality cordons are also adorned with yellow tassels. The red cordon worn by a slim young lady is a typical image of numerous businesses across the country.

Red underwear

33.5x28x0.6cm
Cotton

The lunar calendar that Chinese have been using for thousands of years has a system called the 12 Earthly Branches and 10 Heavenly Stems that are combined to designate years, months, days and hours. There are 12 symbolic animals matching the Earthly Branches and every Chinese is born in a year of a certain animal. The recurrent year – when one reaches 12, 24, 36, etc – is called "*benming nian*" in Chinese. Traditional beliefs say such years are full of potential hazards to a person and one must wear red clothes to fend off the dangers. Though most modern urbanites don't seriously believe in this, they would not offend the ancient wisdom. Thus it is common to see a father sending his son a red belt, a mother binds her daughter's hair with red ribbon, and lovers send each other red underwear. Such red attire must be worn everyday for 365 days. Actually, Chinese people favor the color red since ancient times. This preference is magnified in "*benming nian*". Before the Spring Festival which marks the beginning of a new lunar year, department stores would promote all sorts of things in red like underwear, belt, socks, shoes and outfits. If one desires it, one can be dressed red thoroughly. Liu Xingwu, a prominent contemporary writer, once discussed "*benming nian*" in an article. He argues that psychologically speaking, one reaches a "critical moment" of development upon each "*benming nian*". Xie Fei, a renowned director, also produced a film titled *Benming Nian*. There are customs of paying tribute to the symbolic animal matching the year when one was born, but few take the trouble nowadays. Buying red underwear or a pair of red socks is the most convenient way of going through the "potentially hazardous" year.

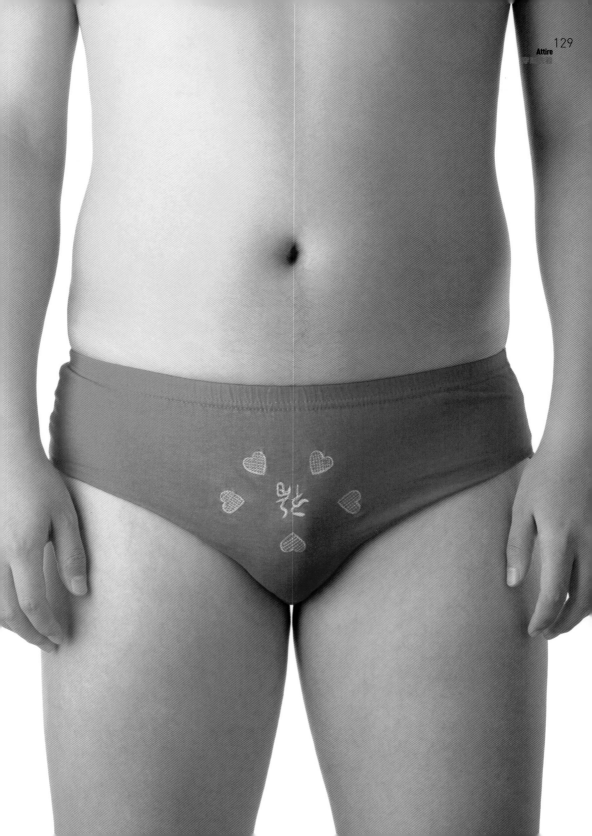

Sun Hat with Face Cover

19x24x20cm
Cotton, Canvas, PVC

In the hot summer, Aunty Wang's best going out accessory is the Sun Hat with Face Cover. It looks like an electric welder's face shield with semicircular hair clasp and a black plastic sheet which can be pull down to cover the face. No one can see Aunty Wang's eyes and facial expressions, the only thing that can be seen is the smooth "black mask" which won't have a negative effect on Aunty Wang's vision but covers her face like a big sun glass that protects her from the ultraviolet rays, wind and dust. In order to protect them from sun and wind and dust, people went through endless ideas, like wearing mouth shades, gauze headscarfs, scarfs and oversleeves, etc. Each sun hat with face cover is multi-functional with hat, mask and sunglass which only cost a few yuan, no wonder it's so popular among people. The likeness of such sun hats might be considered as the expression of love of beauty, though its lack of good taste seems a little bit scary. To protect skin from the sun, the temporary loss of your beautiful look is acceptable. Plus, wearing it is neither dazzling nor troublesome when riding bikes and like nature itself when you pull down the black sheet, no matter what happens outside, you can enjoy you hanging out on the road.

Three-lines badge

6.5x5.9x0.1cm
Plastic

The plastic badge with three red lines is smaller than a grownup's palm. But it is a rare honor among students as only the chief of Young Pioneers can wear it on his or her left arm. The student must excel in study, morality and capabilities such as helping teachers to urge other students to study. Wearing the three-lines plate can be a tough job. Li Yongyu, who has been honored for the second year, says he always empties trash bins on campus and persuades students who throw garbage carelessly to pick litter with him. When someone leaves graffiti on the wall, he would be the first one to clean it. Below the chief of Young Pioneers are the lieutenants and captains who wear badges with two and one lines respectively.

Split pants

43.5x36x1cm
Cotton

Children are enjoying a dazzling array of clothes as fashion industry reaches every corner of modern life. But the split pants still seem to be the uniform of babies and toddlers in the country. Every Chinese, no matter a handsome man or a charming woman, most probably grew up wearing the split pants that reveal the babies' tender buttocks. The popularity of the split pants stems from the practical need of helping the child excrete constantly. There is also a traditional belief that "a child's buttocks carry three fires" – even if a baby wears the split pants in winter, he or she won't catch a cold easily as adults do. The persistence of the split pants also comes from a lack of respect for the babies' privacy. In the West, everyone, including a new-born, enjoys privacy. It might be too serious to link the split pants with privacy, but it's certainly a matter of cultural difference when it comes to split pants and disposable diapers.

Liberation Shoes

26x9.8x9cmx2
Fabric, Rubber

Liberation Shoes are green cloth shoes with rubber sole. Such shoes used to be the standard equipment for the Liberation Army, but many civilians also like to wear the shoes. On May 1, 2003, the army adopted new training shoes. The era of the Liberation Shoes is gone. The official name of such shoes is "cloth shoes with rubber sole". There are many guesses about its popular name. One says that the shoes were first made in the Liberation War before 1949; another simply says they were worn by the Liberation Army. For whatever reason, Liberation Shoes won great popularity among soldiers and civilians in the past half of the 20th century. At times when the nation suffered natural disasters, political turbulences and economic setbacks, there were few other choices than the green military shoes. Even though such shoes look humble, the sole is rather thin and the ventilation is so poor that many suffer from beriberi, a skin disease, such minor problems have not reduced people's attachment to the shoes. In the mushrooming outdoor equipment shops, many young customers choose these shoes, not because of its price or practical function, but more for its political color – just the same as the portrait of Cuban revolutionist Che Guevara. When no more Liberation Shoes are produced by State-owned factories, wearing such shoes display a nostalgia for the old times.

Hotel slippers

27.6x11x0.6cmx2
Non-woven, Foamed plastics

When a woman who seldom travels spent a night in a hotel, she had a lot to say about the disposable utensils: "These simplified, boring and unpractical items are all made of the cheapest and indissolvable plastic. In the hotel rooms, we have lost our individuality." Modern travelers face the dilemma of whether or not they should wear the disposable slippers. Offered in hotels, trains and planes, the slippers seem to be convenient and hygienic. But they cause much pollution and waste. In fact, most slippers are so thin that one feels like walking with bare feet. It's more uncomfortable if the slippers get wet. Many travelers put a pair of their own slippers in the luggage, many hotels also want to become "green" and don't offer disposable items any more.

Drugs and Cosmetics

医药粉黛

Tiger Balm | Yunnan Baiyao | Electronic foot bathing tub | Dabao SOD Lotion | Banlangen | Toilet water |
Itch scratcher | Cupping jar | Scraper | Pot for preparing Chinese medicine | Liuwei Dihuang Pill

Tiger Balm

2.5x2.5x0.9cm
Metal, Medicine

Tiger Balm (Wanjinyou) is a legendary balm for treating headaches, scalds and other minor ailments. It is said that a man named Hu Ziqin left his home in Fujian province of East China and set up a drug store named Yong'antang in Yangon of Burma. His son Hu Wenhu (1882-1954) invented the Tiger Balm, which seemed effective in all sorts of minor ailments. Hu proved to be a smart businessman. He launched promotion campaigns such as "beauty and beast calendar", "tiger car", "new life movement with Tiger Balm" and others that were sensational at the time. Hu also contributed money to build schools and hospitals in China. When Japan invaded China in 1937, the businessman devoted huge sums of money to the fight against invasion. Dubbed as "The King of Tiger Balm", Hu became a much-admired compatriot. Tiger Balm is a perfect example of fragrance treatment. It can instantly wake up one's senses and drive away depression. For many common people, the cheap Tiger Balm is a heaven-sent panacea that promises of fast results. The Tiger Balm has also played a role in foreign relations. Many people in Africa like Tiger Balm. It is said that boxes of the balm can be given as tips or exchanged for small commodities in some African countries. The Chinese often describe someone who seems capable of doing everything but fails to be professional as "Tiger Balm". In today's world, "Tiger Balm" talents are still in demand, though perhaps the demand is not as great as with the real professionals.

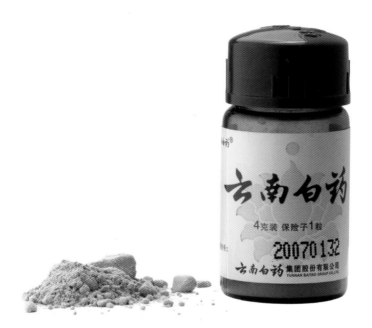

Yunnan Baiyao

4.9x2.1x2.1cm
Glass, Plastic, Medicine

To a certain degree, Baiyao, a white powder for treating hemorrhage, wounds and bruises, is more famous than Yunnan province, where it is produced. Whenever people talk about local products in the southwestern Chinese province, Baiyao is always among the first few items. Qu Huanzhang, a legendary person who lived at the end of the Qing Dynasty (1616-1911), invented the white powder. Dianjun – Yunnan troops – had been equipped with the medicine in their heroic fights against Japanese invaders in the 1930s and 40s. During the Korean War in the 1950s, Premier Zhou Enlai instructed that the best Chinese medicine be sent to the frontline. Millions of bottles of Baiyao were quickly made and sent to the troops. The secret formula of Baiyao now enjoys State protection. For people learning kungfu, getting hurt is inevitable. Having a bottle of Baiyao would bring much confidence to the masters and disciples. In a survey among Western teenagers on their impression of China, topping the list was kungfu. It is said that a Chinese walked down a New York street at night. Three men stopped him. The man gave them some money, but the thugs weren't satisfied. As they raised the fists, the man also raised his arms as an intuitional protection. The thugs yelled: "Kungfu, Chinese kungfu!" and ran away as quickly as possible. They obviously believed that all Chinese are kungfu masters.

Electronic foot bathing tub

42x37.5x22.5cm
Plastic, Metal, etc.

Traditional Chinese medicine holds that the sole of the foot is an epitome of the whole body and that the foot is closely linked with the organs and channels of vital energy. With such medical tradition, Chinese take for granted that giving the feet meticulous care is a daily must. Bathing the feet is like a ceremony. The electronic foot bathing tub can clean the feet and bring multiple enjoyment as it vibrates the water, massages the feet, eliminates viruses, generates fragrant air and provides physiotherapy. This is an ideal present for elderly parents from busy moderns.

Dabao SOD Lotion

13x5.8x3cm
Plastic, SOD, etc.

It is said that SOD is an active organic substance that can prevent ageing by eliminating harmful elements in metabolism. One of Dabao SOD Lotion's advertisements says that the lotion can keep one "white, charming and youthful", hence it is a worthy way to treat one's face. In the cosmetics industry, Dabao is a grassroots name that has won the hearts of millions. Like the Xuehuagao, a milky cream that was popular in the country decades ago, Dabao never puts on an air of importance. Amid the most common washing brands found in any store, Dabao looks very amiable with its affordable price.

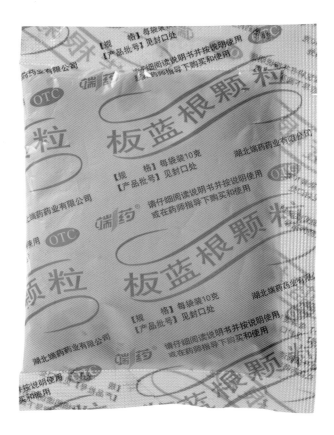

Banlangen

9.5x6.8x0.5cm
Plastic, Medicine

Banlangen, or *Radix Isatidis*, is a Chinese herbal medicine for preventing and treating colds caused by virus. In 2003, when SARS hit Beijing, Hong Kong, Guangzhou and other areas of China, Banlangen was sold out thanks to an unproven rumor that it could prevent the deadly virus. Almost overnight, Banlangen became the most valued medicine. In those days, it was very thoughtful of someone to make a cup of Banlangen for others. Some restaurants also tried to pull back customers by offering Banlangen as tea. Some even prepared soup with Banlangen and pig lungs, which they said would curb coughing and SARS. A popular joke says that when a friend dropped in a family, he said: "Happy New Year. There's not much I can find but two packages of Banlangen. Please accept this humble expression of respect." The host would say: "You are being over-polite. Take a seat. Let's drink two cups of vinegar." In those days, vinegar was also deemed magical for treating SARS. In front of the invisible virus, people felt compelled to take action: fumigating the room with vinegar, putting on a gauze mask when walking outside one's home, drinking a few cups of Banlangen. As SARS slowly receded, Banlangen also resumed its old status of a common treatment for cold. But when the hand-mouth-foot disease took lives of children in the country this year, many kindergartens are again giving the children a cup of Banlangen everyday as a precaution.

Toilet water

24.5x5.5x5.5cm
Glass, Floral oil, Alcohol

Most people use toilet water to keep mosquitoes and other insects away in summer. But years ago, wearing a bit of slightly scented toilet water was almost like putting on the top quality perfume. Da Li, a creative department chief, recalls his happy childhood summer days: "Taking a bath at dusk was a joyful event. I splashed water and always made mom laughing and scolding me. When it was finished, mom would wrap me with a big towel. All the water drops were gone. It was such a refreshed moment. A flock of children smelling of fragrant toilet water would run and frolic in and out of the courtyard. Refreshed, they played joyfully." The summer days in one's childhood memory are full of joy that's scented as toilet water.

Itch scratcher

47.5x3x2.8cm
Bamboo

Itch scratcher is a clever invention. With a hand-shaped head on a long bamboo or wooden stick, the scratcher can reach any place that one's hands can't reach. Tennis player Roger Federer always gets interesting gifts from fans. Once a Chinese fan sent him an itch scratcher. But Federer couldn't figure out its purpose. When he finally learned of its function, Federer was deeply impressed by the Chinese people's wit. In the dry autumn and winter, some elderly people suffer from itchy skin as if ants crawled on their back. Where human hands fail to reach, the itch scratcher proves to be very helpful. The scratcher is also called "*buqiuren*" (not asking others for help) and "*laotoule*" (happy old men), which are apt names. An old saying goes that bitterness and pain are easier to tolerate than sourness and itchiness. With an itch scratcher, one doesn't need to ask anyone else for help. But one must be aware that using the scratcher frequently does no good to the skin. For physical itchiness, a scratcher can deal with it easily. For temptations that keep people's hearts itchy, it's not so easy to find an effective scratcher.

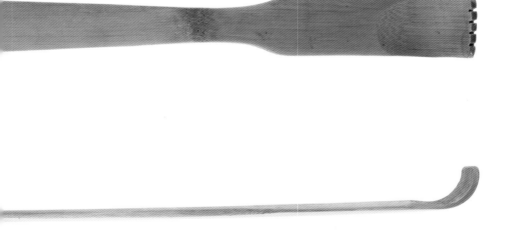

Cupping jar

4.8x4.8x6cm, 6.1x6.1x5.7cm,
8.5x8.5x8.1cm, 9.5x9.5x9.3cm
Glass

Cupping (*ba huo guan*) is a unique treatment for cold, rheumatism, strain of lumbar muscles and other ailments. Practiced for thousands of years in China, it leaves red and purple marks on one's skin. For Westerners, this seems to be evidence of abuse. The air inside the glass cup is consumed with burning paper, making the cup sticking tightly on the strained muscles. As blood rushes to the site, it helps alleviate the symptoms. Some people have got used to cupping regularly to prevent diseases. But the red marks left by cupping can remain for a dozen days, which daunts many people concerned with their public appearance. As Western medicine gains grounds in China, many traditional Chinese doctors have to find other ways to attract people. Cupping is often associated with massage and foot treatment.

Scraper

10x5.3x0.3cm
Ox horn

Scraping (*gua sha*) the patient's neck, chest or back to treat sunstroke and other illnesses would leave many red marks that look like scars. But actually the treatment does no harm to the skin. In just a few days, the skin would resume its normal appearance. Scraping is aimed at increasing micro-circulation of the blood at a certain spot so metabolism can speed up and prevent illnesses. Traditional Chinese medical practices have proved scraping to be effective in encouraging blood circulation, excreting poison, treating sunstroke, alleviating waist and leg strain, reducing tiredness and enhancing the immune system. What is scraped off the body is blood that carries harmful substances from metabolism. Comb, cup covers and other things with a smooth edge can be scrapers. The most ideal scraper is a small board made of ox horn. Director Zheng Xiaolong once made a film called *Guasha Treatment*. A Chinese grandpa scraped his grandson in the United States and the police thought he had abused the child. The seemingly small incident reflects major differences between the West and China in culture, tradition and life.

Pot for preparing Chinese medicine

25x18x18cm
Pottery Clay

After seeing a traditional Chinese doctor, most people choose to send the raw herbal medicine to drug stores or hospitals to turn it into concoction stored in bottles or plastic bags. But most elderly people believe the only correct way to prepare Chinese medicine is to simmer the raw materials in the old pottery pot. For thousands of years, Chinese have followed the same way to treat illnesses. The doctor would look, hear, ask and take pulse before giving a prescription. At the drug store, the druggist wraps the herbal medicine with dark brown paper. Then the patient brings the medicine home to prepare it. Li Shizhen, a great doctor in the Ming Dynasty (1368-1644), said that "medicine prepared in a hurry with wrong water or fire won't have any effect". The quality of preparing medicine is vital to its effect. Every package of medicine can be boiled only twice. Upon the third time, it is believed that the medicine would be harmful. Different from Western medicine, traditional Chinese medicine gives more emphasis on strengthening a patient's vitality than directly dealing with the culprit of the disease. Some weak patients drink a lot of concoction everyday, as if drinking water. They believe that the smell of herbs is more effective than the antiseptic solution in hospitals. Drinking the traditional Chinese medicine is like a ceremony that nurses both the body and the spirit.

Liuwei Dihuang Pill

3x3x3cm
Wax, Medicine

Liuwei Dihuang Pill is known for its effect in strengthening the kidney. Many people think that this traditional Chinese medicine (TCM) can enhance sexuality. But no one wants to let others think that he lacks potency, hence taking the Liuwei Dihuang Pills would need a bit of courage and cover. Actually, this TCM is a nutritional medicine for both man and woman. But most consumers of this pill are still men. Does the Liuwei Dihuang Pill have the same effect as the Viagra? Doctors don't think so, nor do they believe such pills can help with an intercourse. In various medical records, Liuwei Dihuang Pill has been used in some 100 illnesses. But perhaps many people are most concerned with its fabled power on the kidney.

CHINESE STUFF
中国东西

Decoration
装摆饰佩

Bird Nest Ashtray | Fuwa | Amulets featuring Chairman Mao and Premier Zhou | Electronic firecrackers |
Red lantern | Amulet | Electronic painting | Long-life lock | *Pixiu* | Name badge | Double happiness papercut |
Buddhism beads | Plastic flower | Guan Yu

Bird Nest
Ashtray

15x13.6x3.8cm
Glass

Bird Nest became the new labeled national architecture after Beijing Olympic Game. Numbers of tourists visit Bird Nest every day to appreciate the dramatic architecture. Not like the mascota Fuwas, the souvenirs that related to Bird Nest didn't lost fans after Olympic Games, instead, they are popular as always. The Bird Nest ashtray is one of them. The shape of Bird Nest is born to be an ashtray. The hollow part could contain the ashes and the edge can lay cigarettes. Smoking is not an advocated, but placing a Bird Nest ashtray on a tea table in your living room just as collect a mini Bird Nest model – a fascinating functional art work. How to operate sports sites and centers is always a worldwide difficult question after each Olympic Games. As soon as they accomplished their mission of representing the national image, they have a long journey of searching their living. For Chinese people, they don't have such concern. Hanging out to Bird Nest with family and friends occasionally, seeing the architecture which can only be seen on TV and buying some souvenirs related to Bird Nest are the mission of completing the traveling in Beijing.

Fuwa

30x15x10cm
Wool, Lanon

Fuwa are the mascots of the 2008 Beijing Olympics. On Nov 11, 2005, exactly 1,000 days before the Games' opening, the mascots were revealed on a grand ceremony. There are five cute babies: Beibei, a fish from the ocean; Jingjing, a panda from the forest; Huanhuan, a symbol of the Olympic fire; Yingying, a Tibetan antelope from the plateau, and Nini, a swift from the sky. Their colors match those of the five Olympic rings, and their names joint together read "Beijing welcomes you" (*Beijing huanying ni*), which displays the Chinese hospitality very well. The lovely babies have become the brightest stars in 2008, reaching every corner of the world through various media. In Olympic franchise stores, toys and stationery featuring Fuwa are very popular. Many parents would buy Fuwa for their children. Even State leaders bring them on trips as gifts for international counterparts. Some young parents also named their children with Fuwa. In a public place, many children would answer the call "Huanhuan" or other names.

Amulets featuring Chairman Mao and Premier Zhou

40x13x0.4cm
Plastic, Paper, String

Mr Hou put a big badge with Chairman Mao Zedong's portrait on the rearview mirror of his car. The traffic police fined him for obstructing view on the traffic. The man felt he had been wronged and finally got his 50 yuan of fine back. Many drivers like Mr Hou prefer an amulet with Chairman Mao or Premier Zhou Enlai's portrait to protect them. To a certain degree, the two founders of New China have been idolized as gods and perhaps more powerful than gods. While gods only bring certain spiritual comfort, the two leaders of China did bring happy life to the people. In some families, a portrait of Chairman Mao can be seen among calendars of pop stars or the Eight Immortals from folklore. Without a religious belief, many Chinese have found psychological support from the images of national leaders.

Electronic firecrackers

128x9.5x3cm
Plastic, Bulb, etc.

Looking like firecrackers and even sounding like firecrackers, the electronic device is a clever invention that avoids creating the smelly smoke and causing possible fire. More than 2,000 years ago, firecrackers were made to frighten away evil spirits. Today, they are still widely used in weddings, funerals, temple fairs and especially the Spring Festival. But every year, there are many reports about fires and even deaths caused by firecrackers during the Spring Festival. Many people propose banning firecrackers entirely. The government has not banned firecrackers as they hoped. But the electronic firecrackers were invented to suit the needs, as they generate only sound and color, without smoke or pieces of paper. However, such devices cannot meet people's yearning for a genuinely happy festival. Beijing and many other local governments have allowed firecrackers on the rim of the city.

Red lantern

64x53x53cm
Fabric, Plastic, Iron, etc.

It is said that *nian* is a monster that lives deep in the sea. Upon the Eve of the Spring Festival, it crawls onto the beach, eating livestock and men. Thus tradition has it that every family must set off firecrackers, put on red lanterns, stick door guardians' portraits with couplets on the front door, apply red papercuts on windows and do a lot of other things to drive the monster away. Legends never say if the monster still comes out after being frightened for so many Spring Festivals. Today, in big cities across the country, Spring Festival is little more than an occasion of family reunion and a week-long holiday. Few people still write or put on couplets. Red lanterns are also neglected in common families. They are popular only at public places. Besides the Spring Festival, other festive occasions also give ample reason for units to put on a pair of red lanterns on both sides of the door. Zhang Yimou directed the film *Red Lantern* about a feudal family where four wives vied for the master's favor. When the master decided to spend the night at a wife's room, her courtyard would have a pair of red lanterns. In the winter of 2004, many red lanterns were put outside the city council of Paris, as the Year of China was celebrated in France.

Amulet

16.5x4x0.4cm
Cotton

Having a safe journey and survive any dangerous situations are the wishes of everyone. Having an amulet can bring some reassurance to a lonely traveler trekking on a mountain path at night. However modernized life can be, Chinese still have great reverence towards the unknown. Some mothers like to pay tribute to temples. All they wish for is safety and peace. They would get amulets from the temple and give them to every member of the family. This is not a gift of superstition. It is laden with the care of a loving mother. Such a mother is in fact the amulet of the family.

Electronic painting

94.3x55x6.4cm
Glass, Metal, Plastic, etc.

Electronic paintings can revolve and play music. The common people always have an endless resource of inventions, some trying to simplify complicated matters, others doing exactly the opposite. When it is plugged in, the electronic painting will set water flowing and clouds drifting. An advertisement for this funny invention says it "provides a real nature". But perhaps this is the remotest representation of nature in pursuit of visual carnival. However, such paintings are quite popular. In many restaurants and some families' sitting rooms, you can see flowing water on the wall. Like plastic or satin flowers, electronic painting provides a false comfort for people in search of better life.

Long-life lock

32x4.5x2cm
Silver

Sending gifts to a newborn is a difficult thing. Most of the parents have stocked ample formula milk and diapers. Some young people send pretty clothing or toys, but usually these have to wait until the baby is older. Some old people would send the long-life lock, which is a small silver lock bearing words like "100 years of life", "longevity and prosperity", "10,000 years of affluence and prominence". Traditional amulets usually bring good luck and drive away evils. To bring peace of mind, people need something powerful to fend off disturbances from imagined sources. It is said that the Lord of Hell prefers taking lives of the newborn. But when a baby has a long-life lock around its neck upon the first birthday, the Lord of Hell would think the child has been locked and won't take the young life. Every long-life lock carries the parents' best wishes for their offspring.

Pixiu

4.8x2.6x2.7cm
Jade

Pixiu is a mythical animal that only eats and doesn't excrete. For many businessmen, this is a popular symbol for gathering fortune. Niu Kai, a cultural agent, always has a jade *pixiu* pendant around his neck. He believes this will keep his business thriving. *Pixiu* is also a symbol of bravery. Ancient troops would carry flags bearing the image of this mythical animal on the way to battle. But modern people pay more attention to its strong intuition on finding and gathering gold, silver and jewelry. In the past, the emperors said the whole country belonged to them and forbade his imperial ministers to pay tribute to *pixiu* at their homes. But many gambling houses still secretly offered tribute to the legendary animal. Legends say that *pixiu*, dragon, phoenix, tortoise and *qilin* are five auspicious animals. All the ancient mythical animals have become certain symbols in modern society: The dragon and the phoenix symbolize the harmonious life of a newly wed couple; the *qilin* is in charge of sending a son to a family; the tortoise and the crane are symbols of longevity; the *pixiu* is a gatherer and keeper of fortune.

Name badge

3.3x2.1x0.1cm
Plastic

At many scenic spots, you can find peddlers selling rows of small badges bearing Chinese surnames. Tourists who happen to find their own surnames would often spend money for the badge. A name is but a code to identify a person. But people always have enthusiasm to learn about anything related with their names. A human normally lives for less than 100 years, but most people aspire to leave their names for generations to remember. In many Chinese tourist spots, it is common to see visitors carving their names on columns, trees and rocks. The name badge is a souvenir that one can bring home. Lovers, for example, can exchange their name badges as a token of love.

Double happiness papercut

20x25x0.1cm
Paper

Chinese believe in paired "*xi*" (happiness). Various kinds of red papercuts have been made focusing on the Chinese written character. "Double happiness comes to the door" (*shuang xi lin men*) has been a most appropriate wish for various occasions. Many merchants also use this concept to promote their products. Red Double Happiness cigarette, Red Double Happiness table tennis bat and Red Double Happiness insurance are just a few examples. Papercut is a very popular folk art. Double happiness has been the focus of papercut works on all weddings in cities and villages, North and South China. On every betrothal gift and dowry, a double happiness papercut must be put at the most striking place. The cars or sedans that fetch the bride to the wedding banquet and their new home also carry double happiness on the front. The hotel where the banquet is held must also have double happiness on any item, such as the menu, table cloth and others. From the door to the window, the newly weds' room is covered with red papercuts. Double happiness is seen on every gift from friends and relatives. Even a modern digital gadget is packed with red paper that says double happiness. For all Chinese weddings, double happiness is a logo.

Buddhism beads

8x6.5x1.3cm
Wood, Rubber band

Buddhists count beads as they chant sutras. Some beads are put around the neck, others around the wrist or on the belt. Many films depict monks as carrying beads. Monk Sha Wujing in *Journey to the West* carries an awesome bead around his neck, which is composed of human skulls. Most Buddhism beads are made of the Bodhi tree, sandalwood, or some precious stone. Buddhism beads are normally arranged in the numbers of 14, 18, 21, 27, 36, 42, 54, 108 or 1,080, which all carry special meaning in Buddhism. It is believed that chanting sutras while counting beads can reduce worries, improve wisdom and accumulate merits. However, counting beads is still practiced mainly among monks and nuns. The common people, if they wish to adhere to Buddhist doctrines, usually begin with not killing lives, refraining from meat and nurturing benevolent thoughts.

Plastic flower

42x41x41cm
Plastic

In the competition against real flowers, plastic flowers have not lost the battle. The blossoming flowers are charming and fragrant, but they wither quickly and it's not easy to take care of them. The plastic flowers retain their appearance so long as dust doesn't cover them. Li Ka-shing, the Hong Kong billionaire who is probably the richest Chinese in the world, began his business with selling plastic flowers. As technology advances, plastic flowers are made ever more lifelike. Without touching or smelling them, one can hardly distinguish some products from the real ones. But there are many people who can't tolerate fake flowers, as they can't endure anything false. Without the need of nurturing, plastic flowers give you no expectations from budding to flowering. Should the roses in lovers' hands, carnation in mothers' hands and lilies in lovers' hands be replaced with plastic ones, it would be a terrible sight. However vivid the plastic flowers are made, they cannot replace the real ones.

Guan Yu

30.5x17x11.5cm
Porcelain

There are many mortals who have been worshiped as deities in Chinese history. But perhaps the most influential one is Guan Yu, a sworn-in brother of Liu Bei, one of the warlords in the Three Kingdoms Period (AD 220-280). The general, with a crimson face, long beard, green robe and long-handled knife, is worshiped in restaurants, hotels, families of both poor and rich. A main purpose of worshiping the general is to bring more fortunes. It is interesting how Guan's influence is much more profound than that of Liu Bei or any other figures of his time. The early records of Guan didn't give him too much importance. But in succeeding dynasties, the rulers promoted him as a model of upholding feudal morals such as being loyal to the state and the elder brother. Many folk operas also developed centering on the general. They all like to stress how Guan stayed calm reading an ancient book while a doctor cut away poisoned flesh from his arm without anesthesia; how Guan protected Liu Bei's wives and child while they were trapped by Cao Cao; more importantly, how he let Cao Cao go after the Battle at the Red Cliff at the risk of his own life because he must thank Cao for saving him. Confucius is worshiped as the saint of literary achievements, while Guan Yu is revered for martial virtues. Together they form an important part of the Chinese character. Emperor Guangxu, the second but last emperor of feudal China, granted Guan Yu a title of 26 words to praise his virtues.

Index

Office & Classroom

Food & Drink

Eight Treasures Porridge *39*

Gas tank *51*

Pillow cover *65*

Spittoon *76*

Fermented bean curd *40*

Thermos *52*

Bamboo mat *66*

Electric mosquito swatter *78*

Peking chicken roll *41*

Iron pan *54*

Palm-leaf fan *67*

Mosquito incense *79*

Chopsticks *55*

Lunar almanac *68*

Motor tricycle taxi *80*

At Home

Candy box shaped like a golden ingot *56*

Hot water bottle *70*

Mirror *82*

Mutton hotpot *44*

Glass bottles for tea *58*

Piggy bank *71*

Chinese Lazy Susan Table *83*

Sponge gourd brush *46*

Glue roller *60*

Immersion heater *72*

Red envelope *84*

Vegetable scrubber *47*

Rolling pin *61*

Clothes scrubbing board *73*

Spring lock *85*

Small electric oven *48*

Thimble *62*

Suction pump *74*

Cotton Cloth/Plastic Portiere *86*

Honeycomb briquette *50*

Mandarin duck quilt *64*

Scrubbing bath towel *75*

Wooden steelyard *88*

Folding stool *89*

Seat Belt Buckle *90*

White Cat Washing-up Liquid *91*

Purple clay teapot *92*

Dish cover *93*

Bicycle *94*

Mat outside the door *96*

Shower heater *97*

Red-blue-white bag *98*

Leisurely Recreation

Popgun *102*

Glass ball *103*

Disposable cigarette lighter *104*

Chunghwa cigarette *105*

Mahjong *106*

Shuttlecock *107*

Grasshopper cage *108*

Huarongdao puzzle *109*

Military chess *110*

The Shenzhou Spaceship Model *111*

Sandbag *112*

Cloth tiger *113*

Radio *114*

Ornamental walnut *115*

Attire

Safety helmet *118*

Quick tie *119*

Gauze mask *120*

Red scarf *122*

Red sleeve badge *124*

Red cordon *126*

Shoe-pad *127*

Red underwear *128*

Sun Hat with Face Cover *130*

Split pants *132*

Three-lines badge *133*

Liberation Shoes *134*

Hotel slippers *135*

Drugs and Cosmetics

Tiger Balm *138*

Yunnan Baiyao *139*

Electronic foot bathing tub *140*

Dabao SOD Lotion *141*

Banlangen *142*

Toilet water *143*

Itch scratcher *144*

Cupping jar *146*

Scraper *147*

Pot for preparing Chinese medicine *148*

Liuwei Dihuang Pill *149*

Decoration

Bird Nest Ashtray *152*

Fuwa *153*

Amulets featuring Chairman Mao and Premier Zhou *154*

Electronic firecrackers *156*

Red lantern *157*

Amulet *158*

Electronic painting *159*

Long-life lock *160*

Pixiu *161*

Name badge *162*

Double happiness papercut *163*

Buddhism beads *164*

Plastic flower *165*

Guan Yu *166*